THE ULTIMATE TENNIS TRIVIA CHALLENGE

OVER 600 QUIZ QUESTIONS
FOR DIE-HARD TENNIS FANS

HANK PATTON

ISBN: 979-8-89095-054-3

Copyright © 2025 by Curious Press

ALL RIGHTS RESERVED

No part of this book may be reproduced, stored in a retrieval system, or transmitted in any form or by any means, electronic, mechanical, photocopying, recording, scanning, or otherwise, without the prior written permission of the publisher.

CONTENTS

Introduction 1

Chapter 1: Origins and Real Tennis 2
    Chapter 1 Answers 6
    Did You Know? 7

Chapter 2: Lawn Tennis Begins 8
    Chapter 2 Answers 12
    Did You Know? 13

Chapter 3: Early Wimbledon 14
    Chapter 3 Answers 19
    Did You Know? 20

Chapter 4: Early U.S. Open 21
    Chapter 4 Answers 26
    Did You Know? 27

Chapter 5: Early French Open 28
    Chapter 5 Answers 32
    Did You Know? 33

Chapter 6: Early Australian Open 34
    Chapter 6 Answers 38
    Did You Know? 39

Chapter 7: The Davis Cup 40
    Chapter 7 Answers 44
    Did You Know? 45

Chapter 8: Early Olympic Games 46
    Chapter 8 Answers 50

Did You Know?	51
Chapter 9: International Tennis Federation	**52**
Chapter 9 Answers	56
Did You Know?	57
Chapter 10: Early Federation Cup	**58**
Chapter 10 Answers	62
Did You Know?	63
Chapter 11: Early Professional Tours	**64**
Chapter 11 Answers	68
Did You Know?	69
Chapter 12: The 1900s	**70**
Chapter 12 Answers	74
Did You Know?	75
Chapter 13: The 1910s	**76**
Chapter 13 Answers	80
Did You Know?	81
Chapter 14: The 1920s	**82**
Chapter 14 Answers	86
Did You Know?	87
Chapter 15: The 1930s	**88**
Chapter 15 Answers	92
Did You Know?	93
Chapter 16: The 1940s	**94**
Chapter 16 Answers	98
Did You Know?	99
Chapter 17: The 1950s	**100**
Chapter 17 Answers	104
Did You Know?	105
Chapter 18: The 1960s	**106**

Chapter 18 Answers..110
Did You Know? 111

Chapter 19: The 1970s..112
Chapter 19 Answers..116
Did You Know? 117

Chapter 20: The 1980s..118
Chapter 20 Answers..122
Did You Know? 123

Chapter 21: The 1990s..124
Chapter 21 Answers..128
Did You Know? 129

Chapter 22: The 2000s..130
Chapter 22 Answers..134
Did You Know? 135

Chapter 23: The 2010s..136
Chapter 23 Answers..140
Did You Know? 141

Chapter 24: 2020–2024..142
Chapter 24 Answers..146
Did You Know? 147

Chapter 25: Modern Wimbledon 148
Chapter 25 Answers..152
Did You Know? 153

Chapter 26: Modern U.S. Open 154
Chapter 26 Answers..158
Did You Know? 159

Chapter 27: Modern French Open 160
Chapter 27 Answers..164
Did You Know? 165

Chapter 28: Modern Australian Open 166
Chapter 28 Answers 170
Did You Know? 171

Chapter 29: Modern Olympic Tennis 172
Chapter 29 Answers 176
Did You Know? 177

Chapter 30: Modern Davis Cup 178
Chapter 30 Answers 182
Did You Know? 183

Chapter 31: ATP and WTA Finals 184
Chapter 31 Answers 188
Did You Know? 189

Chapter 32: Doubles Records 190
Chapter 32 Answers 194
Did You Know? 195

Chapter 33: Women's Records 196
Chapter 33 Answers 200
Did You Know? 201

Chapter 34: Unbeatable Records 202
Chapter 34 Answers 206
Did You Know? 207

Conclusion 208

ATTENTION:

DO YOU WANT MY FUTURE BOOKS AT HEAVY DISCOUNTS AND EVEN FOR FREE?

HEAD OVER TO WWW.SECRETREADS.COM AND JOIN MY SECRET BOOK CLUB!

INTRODUCTION

Tennis is a sport of elegance, finesse, and power. Players take shots with precision and have captivated spectators around the world for more than 100 years. Whether matches are being played on the grass courts of Wimbledon or the hard courts of the U.S. Open, the game of tennis has delivered some amazing moments during its history.

The game has created legendary players from all over the world, and fans have watched as these great players have made the sport what it is today. This book seeks to challenge your knowledge of tennis, its history, and the players who have risen to the top of its ranks.

With 34 chapters that span the entire history of the game, there are sure to be questions that will catch you with your weight shifted toward the wrong side of the court. You might struggle with the overhead smashes these questions can deliver, but don't worry! Each chapter has an answer section that will give you a bit more information, helping guide you toward a new area of tennis lore to explore.

There will be questions about the biggest Grand Slam moments, questions on the unbeatable records established by the greatest players to ever walk onto the court, and questions dedicated to each decade of the sport's history.

Do you know who has won more Grand Slam titles than any other player? Can you recall the longest match in U.S. Open history? These are just a couple of examples of the kinds of knowledge you'll need to have to get through these pages successfully.

This trivia book is your chance to prove that your tennis love is greater than anyone else's. Show them what you've got and ace these quizzes!

CHAPTER 1:
ORIGINS AND REAL TENNIS

1. The word "tennis" came to the English language from which language in the 14th century?

    A. Spanish
    B. Italian
    C. French
    D. Russian

2. Which knight of King Arthur's round table plays tennis against 17 giants in The Turke and Gowin?

    A. Lancelot
    B. Gawain
    C. Kay
    D. Bors

3. Jeu de paume is thought to be the precursor to tennis, but what did players originally use to hit the ball?

    A. Bats
    B. Paddles
    C. Racquets
    D. Hands

4. Though tennis would eventually split from jeu de paume, the original sport has held a world championship for how many years?

    A. 100
    B. 150
    C. 200
    D. 250

5. Real tennis is the original racquet sport that modern tennis comes from. What is real tennis called in England?

    A. Court tennis
    B. Hall tennis
    C. Royal tennis
    D. Racquet tennis

6. In 1596, a papal legate reported that there were how many indoor tennis courts in Paris?

    A. 250
    B. 300
    C. 350
    D. 400

7. Though other monarchs were associated with real tennis much more closely, which monarch was the first royal to show interest in the game?

   A. Henry V
   B. Henry VI
   C. Henry VII
   D. Henry VIII

8. Henry VIII had a personal tennis court built for himself in which year?

   A. 1511
   B. 1530
   C. 1541
   D. 1547

9. Which of Henry VIII's wives was arrested while watching a game of real tennis?

   A. Anne of Cleves
   B. Catherine Parr
   C. Jane Seymour
   D. Anne Boleyn

10. While James I was reigning in England, how many courts were in London?

    A. 10
    B. 12
    C. 14
    D. 16

11. The first known book about tennis was written by a priest from which country, in 1555?

    A. France
    B. Italy
    C. England
    D. Spain

12. How was King Charles VIII of France's death linked to tennis?

    A. He caught a cold after playing
    B. He was captured by raiders while playing
    C. He hit his head on a door lintel on his way to the court
    D. He suffered a stroke while playing

13. A professional by the name of Forbet was the first to codify a set of rules for real tennis. In which year did he write and publish them?

    A. 1559
    B. 1659
    C. 1599
    D. 1619

14. Which monarch granted a constitution to the Corporation of Tennis Professionals in 1571?

    A. Charles IX
    B. Henry III
    C. Francis II
    D. Francis I

15. Why did real tennis struggle in England during the 17th century?

    A. It was associated with gambling
    B. It was associated with crime rings
    C. It was associated with drug deals
    D. It was associated with anarchist movements

16. The Tennis Court Oath was a key part of which historical moment?

    A. Execution of Charles I
    B. Establishment of Jamestown
    C. English Civil War
    D. French Revolution

17. Germany also had real tennis courts dating back to the 17th century. How many of those courts still exist today?

    A. Zero
    B. One
    C. Two
    D. Six

18. Which of these individuals holds the honor of being the first Real Tennis World Champion?

    A. Raymond Masson
    B. Clergé, The Elder
    C. Joseph Barcellon
    D. Marchisio

Chapter 1 Answers:

1. C. French. It originated from the Anglo-Norman term "tenez," which the serving player likely said to his opponent as the ball was being served.
2. B. Gawain. The story is from around the year 1500, and it is one of the first mentions of the game of tennis.
3. D. Hands. The word "paume" translates to palm, which is what players would use to hit the ball.
4. D. 250. The sport's world championship is the oldest ongoing world championship in any sport.
5. C. Royal tennis. Real tennis is often called "the sport of kings" due to its popularity with monarchs of the past.
6. A. 250. It was a very popular sport, and 250 courts were quite a lot considering the time period.
7. A. Henry V. He reigned from 1413 to 1422, and his interest drove the early popularity of the game in England.
8. B. 1530. His court was built at Hampton Court Palace, though he had several other courts eventually installed at other palaces.
9. D. Anne Boleyn. It is also believed that Henry was playing a game of tennis when he received word of her execution.
10. C. 14. It may not have been growing as quickly as it did in France, but the game was still spreading. James' reign ended in 1625.
11. B. Italy. Antonio Scaino da Salo wrote *Trattato del Giuoco della Palla* during the reign of Henry II, who was an excellent player in France.
12. C. He hit his head on a door lintel on his way to the court. Interestingly, Louis X died from a severe chill after playing.
13. C. 1599. It marked another step forward for the sport, bringing more stability and allowing it to spread.
14. A. Charles IX. The constitution created three levels of professionals: apprentice, associate, and master.
15. A. It was associated with gambling. Many games attracted gamblers to place wagers on outcomes, pushing against the public shift toward puritanism.
16. D. French Revolution. The Oath was a pledge signed by French deputies while they were gathered on a real tennis court, and it was a big early step toward the start of the revolution.
17. A. Zero. Unfortunately, the only evidence of these courts existing back then is thanks to written records.

18. B. Clergé, The Elder. Clergé won the tournament in 1740, but the next World Championship on record didn't take place until 1765.

Did You Know?

The Real Tennis World Champion used to have the right to refuse a challenge from someone looking to dethrone them. Challenges were often turned down based on the amount of prize money offered.

CHAPTER 2:
LAWN TENNIS BEGINS

1. Lawn tennis was invented by Major Walter Clopton Wingfield in which year?

    A. 1860
    B. 1874
    C. 1880
    D. 1890

2. What was the original name given to the game of lawn tennis by Major Wingfield?

    A. Tennis
    B. Sphairistiké
    C. Jeu de paume
    D. Court tennis

3. Where was the first tennis club established?

    A. Wimbledon
    B. Edgbaston
    C. Oxford
    D. Cambridge

4. The All England Croquet Club added lawn tennis to its activities in which year?

    A. 1875
    B. 1877
    C. 1880
    D. 1885

5. In which of these years was the first Wimbledon Championship tournament held?

    A. 1875
    B. 1877
    C. 1880
    D. 1885

6. Who won the first Wimbledon men's singles title?

    A. Spencer Gore
    B. William Renshaw
    C. Reginald Doherty
    D. Laurence Doherty

7. The U.S. National Lawn Tennis Association was founded in which year?

   A. 1875
   B. 1881
   C. 1885
   D. 1890

8. The first U.S. National Championship was held in which year?

   A. 1875
   B. 1881
   C. 1885
   D. 1890

9. The first U.S. National Championship was played at which of these locations?

   A. Newport Casino
   B. Forest Hills
   C. Flushing Meadows
   D. Longwood Cricket Club

10. The first women's singles championship at Wimbledon was held in which year?

    A. 1877
    B. 1884
    C. 1890
    D. 1895

11. Which of these women was the first women's singles champion at Wimbledon?

    A. Lottie Dod
    B. Blanche Bingley
    C. Maud Watson
    D. Charlotte Cooper

12. The first French Championships were held in which year?

    A. 1875
    B. 1881
    C. 1891
    D. 1895

13. The first Australian Championships were held in which year?

A. 1875
B. 1881
C. 1891
D. 1905

14. The first Davis Cup competition was held in which year?

    A. 1890
    B. 1900
    C. 1910
    D. 1920

15. The first Davis Cup competition was held between which two countries?

    A. England and France
    B. England and Australia
    C. United States and England
    D. United States and France

16. The first-ever women's doubles championship at Wimbledon was held in which year?

    A. 1877
    B. 1884
    C. 1899
    D. 1905

17. The first Wimbledon mixed doubles championship was held in which year?

    A. 1877
    B. 1884
    C. 1899
    D. 1905

18. Which of these teams were the first winners of the Wimbledon mixed doubles championship?

    A. Laurence Doherty and Charlotte Cooper
    B. Reginald Doherty and Dorothea Douglass
    C. William Renshaw and Blanche Bingley
    D. Spencer Gore and Maud Watson

Chapter 2 Answers:

1. B. 1874. Major Walter Clopton Wingfield invented lawn tennis in 1874, and he patented the game under the name "Sphairistiké," which was played on an hourglass-shaped court and was designed to be portable, making it easy to set up and play anywhere.
2. B. Sphairistiké. It means "ball-playing" in Greek.
3. B. Edgbaston. The first lawn tennis club was founded in Edgbaston, Warwickshire, marking the beginning of organized lawn tennis clubs.
4. A. 1875. The All England Croquet Club added lawn tennis to its activities in 1875, and this change led to the club eventually becoming the All England Lawn Tennis and Croquet Club.
5. B. 1877. The first Wimbledon Championship was held in 1877, establishing it as the oldest tennis tournament in the world.
6. A. Spencer Gore. The first tournament was held with 22 players, each of whom paid one guinea to participate. Gore won the final against William Marshall.
7. B. 1881. The U.S. National Lawn Tennis Association was founded in 1881 to standardize the rules and organize competitions in the United States.
8. B. 1881. The first U.S. National Championship was held in 1881, with Richard Sears winning the men's singles title.
9. A. Newport Casino. The Newport Casino, located in Newport, Rhode Island, hosted the first U.S. National Championship, which became the precursor to the U.S. Open.
10. B. 1884. The first women's singles championship at Wimbledon was held in 1884, marking the inclusion of women in the prestigious tournament.
11. C. Maud Watson. Maud Watson won the first women's singles championship at Wimbledon in 1884, defeating her sister Lilian Watson in the final.
12. C. 1891. The first French Championships were held in 1891, initially open only to tennis players who were members of French clubs.
13. D. 1905. The first Australian Championships, now known as the Australian Open, were held in 1905 in Melbourne.
14. B. 1900. The first Davis Cup competition was held in 1900, initiated by Dwight F. Davis as a challenge between the United States and Great Britain.

15. C. United States and England. The first Davis Cup competition was held between the United States and England, with the U.S. team emerging victorious.
16. C. 1899. The first Wimbledon women's doubles championship was held in 1899, with Blanche Bingley and Charlotte Cooper winning the title.
17. C. 1899. The first Wimbledon mixed doubles championship was held in 1899, adding another category to the prestigious tournament.
18. A. Laurence Doherty and Charlotte Cooper. Laurence Doherty and Charlotte Cooper won the first Wimbledon mixed doubles championship, showcasing their versatility on the court.

Did You Know?

Walter Clopton Wingfield designed, patented, and manufactured some of the first lawn tennis equipment back in 1873.

CHAPTER 3:
EARLY WIMBLEDON

1. How many matches did defending champion Spencer Gore play in the second edition of the Wimbledon Championship tournament in 1878?

    A. Zero
    B. One
    C. Two
    D. Three

2. Which shot did Frank Hadow effectively introduce to win the second Wimbledon Championship in 1878?

    A. Lob
    B. Volley
    C. Drop
    D. Slice

3. By 1879, just the third iteration of the tournament, how many players participated?

    A. 31
    B. 34
    C. 38
    D. 45

4. Which player became the first Wimbledon champion to defend his crown when he won in 1879 and 1880?

    A. William Renshaw
    B. Ernest Renshaw
    C. John Hartley
    D. Herbert Lawford

5. Maud Watson won the first two women's singles Wimbledon Championships, but who won the third iteration of the tournament in 1886?

    A. Blanche Bingley
    B. Lottie Dod
    C. Blanche Hillyard
    D. Lena Rice

6. How old was Lottie Dod when she won her first women's singles title at Wimbledon in 1887?

    A. 14
    B. 15

C. 16
   D. 17

7. William Renshaw won his seventh men's singles title at Wimbledon in 1889, a mark that would not be beaten until which player did it in 2017?

   A. Pete Sampras
   B. Rafael Nadal
   C. Roger Federer
   D. Novak Djokovic

8. During the 1890 Wimbledon Championships, how many women entered the tournament to compete for the women's singles title?

   A. Four
   B. Eight
   C. 12
   D. 16

9. Which of these years marked the first time that all of the singles and doubles competitions were held concurrently at the Wimbledon Championships?

   A. 1890
   B. 1891
   C. 1892
   D. 1893

10. Which of these teams won the men's doubles competition at Wimbledon in 1894?

    A. Clement Cazalet and George Hillyard
    B. C.O.S. Hatton and Leslie Hausburg
    C. Harry Barlow and C.H. Martin
    D. Herbert and Wilfred Baddeley

11. Which country provided Wimbledon with its first royal visitors during the 1895 Championships?

    A. England
    B. Austria
    C. France
    D. Spain

12. Which Wimbledon Championship tournament was the first to introduce the All England Plate?

A. 1894
   B. 1895
   C. 1896
   D. 1899

13. Reginald Doherty won the 1900 men's singles tournament at Wimbledon. Who did he defeat in the final?

   A. Sydney Smith
   B. Arthur Gore
   C. Harold Nisbet
   D. Laurence Doherty

14. Muriel Robb won the only match in Wimbledon history that had which of these characteristics?

   A. It ended early due to the weather
   B. It was canceled and restarted the next day
   C. It was played in pouring rain
   D. It was played in the early morning

15. Which of these sports equipment companies supplied the balls and equipment for the 1904 Wimbledon Championships?

   A. Titleist
   B. Wilson
   C. Prince
   D. Slazenger

16. May Sutton was the first Wimbledon winner from which country?

   A. Scotland
   B. Australia
   C. Canada
   D. United States

17. The 1907 Wimbledon Championships marked the first time the Centre Court received which of these treatments?

   A. It was mowed with a gas lawnmower
   B. It was protected by a tarpaulin cover
   C. It was painted with white paint between each match
   D. A new type of ryegrass was used

18. The first women's doubles championship at Wimbledon was held in 1913. Who were the runners-up?

A. Dora Boothby and Winifred McNair
B. Dorothea Lambert Chambers and Charlotte Cooper Sterry
C. Ethel Larcombe and Mabel Parton
D. Mrs. Armstrong and Olive Manser

Chapter 3 Answers:

1. B. One. As the defending champion at the time, Gore was only required to play against whoever emerged as the winner of the all-comers' final.
2. A. Lob. Hadow needed a way to counter Gore's volleys, and he found the lob an effective way to control the pace of the match.
3. D. 45. Of those 45 players in the 1879 Wimbledon Championship, 36 were competing in their first Wimbledon.
4. C. John Hartley. Though Hartley was the first to win two in a row, his accomplishment would be dwarfed by William Renshaw over the next few years.
5. A. Blanche Bingley. Though Bingley would be successful in 1886, Lottie Dod would win the next two women's singles championships at Wimbledon.
6. B. 15. To be precise, she was 15 years and 285 days old when she won the 1887 women's singles title, and she remains the youngest women's singles champion in Wimbledon history.
7. C. Roger Federer. Roger's Wimbledon win in 2017 was his eighth, making him the first man in tennis history to reach that mark.
8. A. Four. Out of any women's singles competition at Wimbledon, the 1890 iteration holds the record for the fewest entrants ever.
9. C. 1892. Before this year, the men's singles tournament was held before the doubles and women's singles tournaments.
10. D. Herbert and Wilfred Baddeley. They defeated Harry Barlow and C.H. Martin in the final, even though they fell behind 1–0 and 2–1 in sets.
11. B. Austria. Princess Stephanie of Belgium and Prince Edmund Batthyany-Strattmann were in attendance for the men's doubles challenge rounds.
12. C. 1896. It was a second competition for players who were eliminated in the first and second rounds of the main tournament. It was discontinued after almost 100 years of competition.
13. A. Sydney Smith. Doherty and his brother Laurence also went on to win the doubles title that year, the final year with Queen Victoria as the monarch of England.
14. B. It was canceled and restarted the next day. Robb was tied with Charlotte Cooper Sterry one set to one when the match was canceled and restarted fresh the next day.

15. D. Slazenger. Though they are more known for golf equipment today, they were early partners for the game of tennis.
16. D. United States. Not only was Sutton the first American winner but she was also the first winner to come from overseas.
17. B. It was protected by a tarpaulin cover. The grounds crew was slowly making improvements and upping the quality of the court.
18. B. Dorothea Lambert Chambers and Charlotte Cooper Sterry. A total of 21 teams entered the first women's doubles tournament, a strong showing for the new event.

Did You Know?

Wimbledon was televised for the first time back in 1937.

CHAPTER 4:
EARLY U.S. OPEN

1. How many players entered the first U.S. Open in 1881?

   A. Four
   B. 12
   C. 20
   D. 25

2. Richard Sears was the men's singles U.S. Open champion every year from 1881 until which year, when he relinquished the crown?

   A. 1885
   B. 1886
   C. 1887
   D. 1888

3. The first U.S. Open to hold a women's singles championship was in 1887—who won that first tournament?

   A. Laura Knight
   B. Ellen Hansell
   C. Helen Day Harris
   D. Alice Janney

4. Women's doubles was added to the U.S. Open in 1889. Which of these women won the singles and doubles tournaments that year?

   A. Lida Voorhees
   B. Grace Roosevelt
   C. Bertha Townsend
   D. Margarette Ballard

5. Mabel Cahill was the first non-American to win the women's singles crown at the 1891 U.S. Open. Which country did she represent?

   A. England
   B. Ireland
   C. Scotland
   D. Canada

6. Mabel Cahill won three crowns in 1892 when mixed doubles was played for the first time at the U.S. Open. Who was her mixed doubles partner?

   A. Clarence Hobart
   B. Bob Huntington
   C. Oliver Campbell
   D. Fred Hovey

7. Robert Wrenn won four U.S. Open singles titles in total, but one player prevented him from winning three in a row in 1895. Who was it?

    A. William Larned
    B. Oliver Campbell
    C. Malcolm Whitman
    D. Frederick Hovey

8. Juliette Atkinson won five straight women's doubles titles at the U.S Open, but how many different partners did she have to win those five titles?

    A. One
    B. Two
    C. Three
    D. Four

9. In 1902, the men's doubles title at the U.S. Open was won by a pair of players from which of these countries?

    A. Ireland
    B. Great Britain
    C. United States
    D. France

10. In 1903, Laurence Doherty of Great Britain became the first British player to win the men's singles title at the U.S. Open by defeating which player in the final?

    A. William Larned
    B. Harry Allen
    C. Holcombe Ward
    D. Beals Wright

11. Which player only captured one U.S. Open men's singles title in 1904, though he also won the men's doubles title that same year?

    A. Maurice McLoughlin
    B. William Clothier
    C. Beals Wright
    D. Holcombe Ward

12. William Larned won two men's singles titles in 1901 and 1902, then he won again in 1907. How many did he win in a row, beginning in 1907?

A. Two
   B. Three
   C. Four
   D. Five

13. Hazel Hotchkiss Wightman won her first U.S. Open women's singles title in 1909. How many more did she win after that?

    A. Two
    B. Three
    C. Four
    D. Five

14. Which year of U.S. Open competition saw the end of the Challenge Round, forcing the defending champion to enter the main bracket with the rest of the competitors?

    A. 1910
    B. 1911
    C. 1912
    D. 1913

15. Maurice McLoughlin reached the U.S. Open men's singles final how many times in a row beginning in 1911?

    A. Three
    B. Four
    C. Five
    D. Six

16. R. Norris Williams won the 1916 men's singles title at the U.S. Open, defeating which opponent in the final?

    A. William Johnson
    B. Robert Lindley Murray
    C. Clarence Griffin
    D. Watson Washburn

17. Molla Bjurstedt of Norway won the women's singles title how many times in a row?

    A. Two
    B. Three
    C. Four
    D. Five

18. Which year saw the U.S. Open's men's tournaments held in Forest Hills, New York, after moving from Rhode Island?

    A. 1915
    B. 1916
    C. 1917
    D. 1918

Chapter 4 Answers:

1. D. 25. Richard Sears emerged victorious at the end of the tournament, defeating William Glyn in the final.
2. D. 1888. Henry Slocum emerged from the All Comers' finals, but Richard Sears did not compete in the Challenge Round, as he had retired from the sport.
3. B. Ellen Hansell. Though there were only seven entrants for the first women's singles championship at the U.S. Open, Hansell emerged victorious.
4. C. Bertha Townsend. She was the defending singles champion at the time, so she only had to compete in the Challenge Round to win the singles crown once again.
5. B. Ireland. Cahill defeated Grace Roosevelt in the All Comers' final, then defeated Ellen Roosevelt in the Challenge Round to capture the championship.
6. A. Clarence Hobart. They defeated Elisabeth Moore and Rodmond V. Beach in straight sets to capture the first mixed doubles championship at the U.S. Open.
7. D. Frederick Hovey. Hovey defeated Wrenn in straight sets for his only singles title.
8. C. Three. Atkinson won titles with Helen Hellwig, Elisabeth Moore, and Kathleen Atkinson.
9. B. Great Britain. Reginald and Laurence Doherty, after experiencing great success at Wimbledon, began experiencing success in the United States.
10. A. William Larned. Doherty defeated Larned in straight sets, though he needed tiebreakers to win the final set 10–8.
11. D. Holcombe Ward. Ward won a total of six men's doubles titles at the U.S. Open with two different partners.
12. D. Five. Larned won each U.S. Open men's singles title from 1907 to 1911, an impressive run considering he went four years without winning after his first two.
13. B. Three. She won the first three in a row, then she snagged one more in 1919 toward the end of her career.
14. C. 1912. It only took one year for the defending champion to prove that playing through the bracket was not too much of an issue.
15. C. Five times. McLoughlin only won two of those five trips to the final, and each one of those trips included playing through the entire bracket with the elimination of the Challenge Round.

16. A. William Johnson. Williams fell behind 1-0 and 2-1 in sets but managed to complete the comeback and win the title.
17. C. Four. Bjurstedt was able to benefit from the Challenge Round for each of her consecutive wins, and she lost in the semifinals in a bid for her fifth win.
18. A. 1915. The move happened after around 100 tennis players signed a petition in favor of the move. They thought it would be better for the players and sport in terms of travel and popularity with fans.

Did You Know?

Newport Casino, in Newport, Rhode Island, was the first venue to host the U.S. Open.

CHAPTER 5:
EARLY FRENCH OPEN

1. In which of these years was the first French Open?

    A. 1881
    B. 1891
    C. 1901
    D. 1911

2. Who won the first-ever men's singles title at the French Open?

    A. H. Briggs
    B. Paul Ayme
    C. Max Décugis
    D. René Lacoste

3. The first women's singles tournament at the French Open was held in which year?

    A. 1897
    B. 1907
    C. 1917
    D. 1927

4. How many players participated in the first women's singles tournament at the French Open?

    A. Two
    B. Four
    C. Eight
    D. 16

5. Which surface was used for the French Open from 1891 to 1907?

    A. Grass
    B. Clay
    C. Sand
    D. Hard

6. Who was the first non-French player to win the men's singles title at the French Open?

    A. H. Briggs
    B. Paul Ayme
    C. Max Décugis
    D. René Lacoste

7. In which year was the mixed doubles event added to the French Open?

A. 1902
B. 1912
C. 1922
D. 1932

8. The French Open became an international event in which year, allowing non-French club members to compete?

    A. 1905
    B. 1915
    C. 1925
    D. 1935

9. Who won the first women's singles title at the French Open in 1897?

    A. Adine Masson
    B. Suzanne Lenglen
    C. Simonne Mathieu
    D. Françoise Durr

10. The French Open moved to its current location, Stade Roland Garros, in which year?

    A. 1918
    B. 1928
    C. 1938
    D. 1948

11. Which player won the most men's singles titles at the French Open before the Open Era?

    A. Max Décugis
    B. Henri Cochet
    C. René Lacoste
    D. Jean Borotra

12. The French Open was not held during which major global event?

    A. World War I
    B. World War II
    C. The Great Depression
    D. The Cold War

13. Who won the men's singles title at the French Open in 1914, just before World War I?

    A. William Laurentz
    B. Jean Samazeuilh

- C. André Gobert
- D. Max Décugis

14. Which player won the women's singles title at the French Open in 1914?

    - A. Suzanne Lenglen
    - B. Jeanne Matthey
    - C. Marguerite Broquedis
    - D. Adine Masson

15. How many times did Adine Masson win the women's singles title at the French Open?

    - A. Two
    - B. Three
    - C. Four
    - D. Five

16. Who won the men's singles title at the French Open in 1920?

    - A. Jean Samazeuilh
    - B. André Gobert
    - C. William Laurentz
    - D. Max Décugis

17. Which player won the women's singles title at the French Open in 1920?

    - A. Suzanne Lenglen
    - B. Jeanne Matthey
    - C. Marguerite Broquedis
    - D. Adine Masson

18. The French Open was held at which venue before moving to Stade Roland Garros?

    - A. Tennis Club de Paris
    - B. Stade Français
    - C. Croix-Catelan
    - D. Société Athlétique de la Villa Primrose

Chapter 5 Answers:

1. B. 1891. The French Open was first held in 1891 and was initially open only to players who were members of French clubs. This marked the beginning of what would become one of the four Grand Slam tournaments.
2. A. H. Briggs. Briggs, a Briton who resided in Paris, won the first men's singles title. His victory highlighted the early international influence on the tournament.
3. A. 1897. The first women's singles tournament at the French Open was held in 1897, reflecting the growing inclusion of women in competitive tennis.
4. B. Four. There were only four entries in the first women's singles tournament, indicating the modest beginnings of women's participation in the event.
5. C. Sand. The French Open was played on sand from 1892 to 1907, before switching to the clay courts that it is famous for today.
6. A. H. Briggs. Briggs was the first non-French player to win the men's singles title, setting a precedent for international competitors.
7. A. 1902. The mixed doubles event was added to the French Open in 1902, expanding the tournament's format and providing more opportunities for players.
8. C. 1925. The French Open became an international event in 1925, allowing non-French club members to compete and significantly increasing the tournament's prestige.
9. A. Adine Masson. Masson won the first women's singles title in 1897, becoming a pioneer for women's tennis in France.
10. B. 1928. The French Open moved to Stade Roland Garros in 1928, providing a permanent home for the tournament and enhancing its facilities.
11. A. Max Décugis. Décugis won eight men's singles titles before the Open Era, making him one of the most successful players in the tournament's early history.
12. A. World War I. The French Open was not held from 1915 to 1919 due to World War I, reflecting the impact of global events on sports.
13. D. Max Décugis. Décugis won the men's singles title in 1914, just before World War I interrupted the tournament.
14. C. Marguerite Broquedis. Broquedis won the women's singles title in 1914, showcasing her talent in the final tournament before the war.

15. B. Three times. Adine Masson won the women's singles title three times, establishing herself as a dominant player in the early years of the French Open.
16. B. André Gobert. Gobert won the men's singles title in 1920, marking a successful return of the tournament after World War I.
17. A. Suzanne Lenglen. Lenglen won the women's singles title in 1920, beginning her legendary career at the French Open.
18. C. Croix-Catelan. The French Open was held at Croix-Catelan, providing a historical backdrop to the tournament's early years, before it was moved to Stade Roland Garros.

Did You Know?

Both the French Open tournament and venue are named after the French aviator Roland Garros.

CHAPTER 6:
EARLY AUSTRALIAN OPEN

1. In which year was the first Australian Open held?

    A. 1900
    B. 1905
    C. 1910
    D. 1915

2. Who won the first men's singles title at the Australian Open in 1905?

    A. Anthony Wilding
    B. Rodney Heath
    C. Norman Brookes
    D. Gerald Patterson

3. The first women's singles tournament at the Australian Open was held in which year?

    A. 1920
    B. 1922
    C. 1924
    D. 1926

4. How many players participated in the first men's singles tournament at the Australian Open?

    A. Eight
    B. 16
    C. 32
    D. 64

5. Which surface was used for the Australian Open from its inception until 1987?

    A. Grass
    B. Clay
    C. Hard
    D. Carpet

6. Who was the first non-Australian player to win the men's singles title at the Australian Open?

    A. Anthony Wilding
    B. Norman Brookes
    C. Fred Alexander
    D. Gerald Patterson

7. In which year was the mixed doubles event added to the Australian Open?

    A. 1920
    B. 1922
    C. 1924
    D. 1926

8. The Australian Open became an international event in which year, allowing non-Australian players to compete?

    A. 1920
    B. 1925
    C. 1930
    D. 1935

9. Who won the first women's singles title at the Australian Open in 1922?

    A. Daphne Akhurst
    B. Esna Boyd
    C. Sylvia Lance Harper
    D. Margaret Molesworth

10. The Australian Open moved to its current location, Melbourne Park, in which year?

    A. 1972
    B. 1988
    C. 1996
    D. 2000

11. Which player won the most men's singles titles at the Australian Open before the Open Era?

    A. Jack Crawford
    B. Norman Brookes
    C. Gerald Patterson
    D. Roy Emerson

12. The Australian Open was not held during which major global event?

    A. World War I
    B. World War II
    C. The Great Depression
    D. The Cold War

13. Who won the men's singles title at the Australian Open in 1935?

    A. Jack Crawford
    B. Fred Perry
    C. Pat O'Hara Wood
    D. Gerald Patterson

14. Which player won the women's singles title at the Australian Open in 1935?

    A. Daphne Akhurst
    B. Joan Hartigan
    C. Dorothy Round
    D. Nancye Wynne

15. How many times did Daphne Akhurst win the women's singles title at the Australian Open?

    A. Two
    B. Three
    C. Four
    D. Five

16. Who won the men's singles title at the Australian Open in 1920?

    A. Pat O'Hara Wood
    B. Gerald Patterson
    C. James Anderson
    D. Norman Brookes

17. Which player won the women's singles title at the Australian Open in 1920?

    A. Daphne Akhurst
    B. Esna Boyd
    C. Sylvia Lance Harper
    D. Margaret Molesworth

18. The Australian Open was held at which venue before moving to Melbourne Park?

    A. Kooyong Stadium
    B. Albert Reserve
    C. White City Stadium
    D. Royal Sydney Golf Club

Chapter 6 Answers:

1. B. 1905. The Australian Open was first held in 1905, originally known as the Australasian Championships. It was created to promote tennis in Australia and New Zealand, and it has since evolved into one of the four Grand Slam tournaments.
2. B. Rodney Heath. Heath won the first men's singles title at the Australian Open, defeating Arthur Curtis in the final.
3. B. 1922. The first women's singles tournament at the Australian Open was held in 1922, marking a significant step toward gender equality in tennis.
4. A. Eight. There were only eight players in the first men's singles tournament. This small field highlighted the humble beginnings of what would become a major tennis event.
5. A. Grass. The Australian Open was played on grass courts until 1987, which was typical for major tennis tournaments at the time. The switch to hard courts occurred in 1988, modernizing the tournament and improving playing conditions.
6. A. Anthony Wilding. Wilding, a New Zealander, was the first non-Australian player to win the men's singles title in 1909. His victory highlighted the growing international appeal of the tournament and set a precedent for future international champions.
7. B. 1922. The mixed doubles event was added to the Australian Open in 1922, providing more opportunities for players to compete and showcasing the versatility of tennis athletes.
8. B. 1925. The Australian Open became an international event in 1925, allowing non-Australian players to compete. This change helped elevate the tournament's status on the global stage.
9. D. Margaret Molesworth. Molesworth won the first women's singles title in 1922, defeating Esna Boyd in the final. Her victory was a milestone for women's tennis in Australia.
10. B. 1988. The Australian Open moved to Melbourne Park in 1988, transitioning from grass to hard courts. This move helped increase the event's popularity.
11. A. Jack Crawford. Crawford won six men's singles titles before the Open Era, dominating the tournament during the 1930s. His achievements contributed to the Australian Open's rich history and established him as one of the greatest players of his time.
12. B. World War II. The Australian Open was not held from 1941 to 1945 due to World War II, reflecting the global impact of the conflict on

sports and other activities. The interruption highlighted the challenges faced by athletes during wartime.
13. A. Jack Crawford. Crawford won the men's singles title in 1935, adding to his impressive record. He defeated Fred Perry in the final, showcasing his skill and determination. Crawford's victory was part of his remarkable career in tennis.
14. C. Dorothy Round. Round won the women's singles title in 1935, becoming one of the few international champions of the era. Her victory demonstrated the growing competitiveness of the tournament and her exceptional talent.
15. D. Five times. Daphne Akhurst won the women's singles title five times, from 1925 to 1930. Her consistent performance established her as one of the greatest players in Australian Open history and set a high standard for future champions.
16. A. Pat O'Hara Wood. Wood won the men's singles title in 1920, defeating Ronald Thomas in the final. His victory was part of a successful career in Australian tennis and contributed to the tournament's early prestige.
17. D. Margaret Molesworth. Molesworth won the women's singles title in 1920, defending her title from the previous year. Her back-to-back victories solidified her status as a top player and highlighted her dominance in the early years of the tournament.
18. A. Kooyong Stadium. The Australian Open was held at Kooyong Stadium before moving to Melbourne Park. Kooyong was the venue for the tournament from 1972 to 1987, providing a historical backdrop to the event's development.

Did You Know?

The Warehouseman's Cricket Ground in Melbourne hosted the first Australian Open in 1905. It is now called the Albert Reserve Tennis Centre.

CHAPTER 7:
THE DAVIS CUP

1. In which year was the first Davis Cup held?

    A. 1890
    B. 1900
    C. 1910
    D. 1920

2. Who founded the Davis Cup competition?

    A. James Dwight
    B. William Larned
    C. Dwight F. Davis
    D. Harold Mahony

3. Which two countries competed in the first Davis Cup match?

    A. United States and France
    B. Great Britain and Australia
    C. United States and Great Britain
    D. France and Belgium

4. Where was the first Davis Cup match held?

    A. Wimbledon
    B. Longwood Cricket Club
    C. Kooyong Stadium
    D. Stade Roland Garros

5. Who won the first Davis Cup match?

    A. United States
    B. Great Britain
    C. Australia
    D. France

6. Which country won the Davis Cup in 1904, marking the first victory outside of the United States and Great Britain?

    A. France
    B. Belgium
    C. Australasia
    D. Germany

7. How many teams competed in the Davis Cup by 1913?

    A. Four
    B. Eight
    C. 12
    D. 16

8. The Davis Cup was not held during which major global event?

   A. World War I
   B. World War II
   C. The Great Depression
   D. The Cold War

9. Who won the Davis Cup in 1920, marking the first victory for a European country other than Great Britain?

   A. France
   B. Belgium
   C. Germany
   D. Spain

10. Which country dominated the Davis Cup during the 1920s, winning six titles?

    A. United States
    B. France
    C. Australia
    D. Great Britain

11. Who was the captain of the United States team that won the Davis Cup in 1927?

    A. Bill Tilden
    B. Dwight F. Davis
    C. William Johnston
    D. Vincent Richards

12. The Davis Cup format changed in 1923 to include which new feature?

    A. Knockout rounds
    B. Round-robin play
    C. Challenge Round
    D. Group stages

13. Which country won the Davis Cup in 1930, ending the United States' dominance?

    A. France
    B. Australia
    C. Great Britain
    D. Germany

14. Who was the first player to win the Davis Cup as both a player and captain?

    A. Bill Tilden
    B. René Lacoste
    C. Henri Cochet
    D. Fred Perry

15. How many times did the United States win the Davis Cup between 1900 and 1930?

    A. Five
    B. Ten
    C. 15
    D. 20

16. Which country won the Davis Cup in 1922, marking their first victory?

    A. France
    B. Australia
    C. Belgium
    D. Spain

17. The Davis Cup trophy was designed by which player?

    A. Dwight F. Davis
    B. Bill Tilden
    C. William Larned
    D. Harold Mahony

18. The Davis Cup was originally known by what name?

    A. International Tennis Challenge
    B. World Tennis Championship
    C. International Lawn Tennis Challenge
    D. Global Tennis Cup

Chapter 7 Answers:

1. B. 1900. The Davis Cup was created to foster international competition in tennis.
2. C. Dwight F. Davis. Dwight F. Davis, a Harvard University student, founded the Davis Cup and designed the tournament format.
3. C. United States and Great Britain. This match set the stage for the long-standing rivalry between the two nations in tennis.
4. B. Longwood Cricket Club. The first Davis Cup match was held at Longwood Cricket Club in Boston, Massachusetts. This venue was chosen for its excellent grass courts.
5. A. United States. The United States won the first Davis Cup match in 1900, defeating Great Britain 3-0. This victory helped establish the United States as a strong contender in international tennis.
6. C. Australasia. Australasia (a combined team of Australia and New Zealand) won the Davis Cup in 1907, marking the first victory outside of the United States and Great Britain. This team showcased the growing talent in the Southern Hemisphere.
7. B. Eight. By 1913, eight teams were competing in the Davis Cup, reflecting the growing popularity of the tournament. The expansion included teams from Europe and the Americas.
8. A. World War I. The Davis Cup was not held from 1915 to 1918 due to World War I. The interruption highlighted the impact of global events on sports.
9. B. Belgium. Belgium won the Davis Cup in 1920, marking the first victory for a European country other than Great Britain. This win demonstrated the increasing competitiveness of European tennis.
10. A. United States. The United States dominated the Davis Cup during the 1920s, winning six titles. This period was marked by the exceptional performance of players like Bill Tilden.
11. A. Bill Tilden. Bill Tilden was the captain of the United States team that won the Davis Cup in 1927. Tilden was known for his powerful serve and strategic play.
12. C. Challenge Round. The Davis Cup format changed in 1923 to include the Challenge Round, where the defending champion automatically qualified for the final. This format aimed to give the reigning champions an advantage.
13. A. France. France won the Davis Cup in 1930, ending the United States' dominance. The French team included legendary players like René Lacoste and Henri Cochet.

14. B. René Lacoste. René Lacoste was the first player to win the Davis Cup as both a player and captain. Lacoste was also known for his contributions to tennis fashion, including the invention of the polo shirt.
15. B. Ten times. The United States won the Davis Cup ten times between 1900 and 1930. This impressive record underscored the country's dominance in early Davis Cup history.
16. B. Australia. Australia won the Davis Cup in 1922, marking their first victory. This win helped establish Australia as a major force in international tennis.
17. A. Dwight F. Davis. Dwight F. Davis designed the Davis Cup trophy, which is made of sterling silver. The trophy has become one of the most iconic symbols in tennis.
18. C. International Lawn Tennis Challenge. The name was later changed to honor its founder, Dwight F. Davis.

Did You Know?

Though the Davis Cup was first held in 1900, international team competitions were taking place for several years before the Davis Cup was formed.

CHAPTER 8:
EARLY OLYMPIC GAMES

1. In which year was tennis first included in the Summer Olympics?

    A. 1896
    B. 1900
    C. 1904
    D. 1908

2. Who won the first men's singles gold medal in tennis at the 1896 Olympics?

    A. John Pius Boland
    B. Dionysios Kasdaglis
    C. Edwin Flack
    D. Friedrich Traun

3. The first women's singles tennis competition at the Olympics was held in which year?

    A. 1900
    B. 1904
    C. 1908
    D. 1912

4. How many players participated in the first women's singles tennis competition at the Olympics?

    A. Two
    B. Four
    C. Six
    D. 12

5. Which surface was used for tennis competitions at the 1908 London Olympics?

    A. Grass
    B. Clay
    C. Hard
    D. Carpet

6. Who was the first female tennis player to win an Olympic gold medal?

    A. Charlotte Cooper Sterry
    B. Suzanne Lenglen
    C. Helen Wills
    D. Dorothea Lambert Chambers

7. Tennis was excluded from the Olympics after which year due to disputes over amateur versus professional players?

    A. 1920
    B. 1924
    C. 1928
    D. 1932

8. The mixed doubles event was first included in the Olympics in which year?

    A. 1896
    B. 1900
    C. 1904
    D. 1908

9. Who won the men's singles gold medal at the 1920 Antwerp Olympics?

    A. Randolph Lycett
    B. Charles Winslow
    C. Ichiya Kumagae
    D. Louis Raymond

10. Which country dominated tennis at the 1924 Paris Olympics, winning multiple medals?

    A. United States
    B. France
    C. Great Britain
    D. Australia

11. Who won the women's singles gold medal at the 1924 Paris Olympics?

    A. Helen Wills
    B. Suzanne Lenglen
    C. Elizabeth Ryan
    D. Kitty McKane

12. Tennis returned to the Olympics as a demonstration sport in which year?

    A. 1964
    B. 1968
    C. 1972
    D. 1976

13. Who won the men's singles gold medal at the 1968 Mexico City Olympics, though it was still a demonstration event?

    A. Manuel Santana
    B. John Newcombe
    C. Rafael Osuna
    D. Roy Emerson

14. Which player won the women's singles gold medal at the 1968 Mexico City Olympics demonstration event?

    A. Billie Jean King
    B. Margaret Court
    C. Ann Jones
    D. Virginia Wade

15. How many times did tennis appear as a full medal sport at the Olympics before 1970?

    A. Three
    B. Four
    C. Five
    D. Six

16. Who was the first player to win both singles and doubles gold medals at the same Olympics?

    A. John Pius Boland
    B. Charlotte Cooper Sterry
    C. Helen Wills
    D. Suzanne Lenglen

17. Which country won the most tennis medals at the Olympics before 1970?

    A. United States
    B. Great Britain
    C. France
    D. Australia

18. Tennis was played on which type of court surface at the 1924 Paris Olympics?

    A. Grass
    B. Clay
    C. Hard
    D. Carpet

Chapter 8 Answers:

1. A. 1896. Tennis was first included in the Summer Olympics in 1896, held in Athens. It was one of the nine sports featured in the inaugural Games.
2. A. John Pius Boland. Boland, an Irish player, won the first men's singles gold medal in tennis at the 1896 Olympics. He also won the men's doubles event.
3. A. 1900. The first women's singles tennis competition at the Olympics was held in 1900 in Paris, marking the debut of women in Olympic tennis.
4. B. Four. There were only four players in the first women's singles tennis competition at the 1900 Olympics, reflecting the early stages of women's participation in the sport.
5. A. Grass. Tennis competitions at the 1908 London Olympics were played on grass courts, which were typical for major tennis tournaments at the time.
6. A. Charlotte Cooper Sterry. Cooper Sterry was the first female tennis player to win an Olympic gold medal, achieving this feat at the 1900 Paris Olympics.
7. B. 1924. Tennis was excluded from the Olympics after the 1924 Paris Games due to disputes between the International Lawn Tennis Federation and the International Olympic Committee over amateurism.
8. B. 1900. The mixed doubles event was first included in the Olympics in 1900, allowing male and female players to compete together.
9. D. Louis Raymond. Raymond, a South African player, won the men's singles gold medal at the 1920 Antwerp Olympics.
10. A. United States. The United States dominated tennis at the 1924 Paris Olympics, winning multiple medals in both singles and doubles events.
11. A. Helen Wills. Wills won the women's singles gold medal at the 1924 Paris Olympics, showcasing her exceptional talent and solidifying her status as a tennis legend.
12. B. 1968. Tennis returned to the Olympics as a demonstration sport in 1968 at the Mexico City Games, with an age limit of under 21.
13. C. Rafael Osuna. Osuna, a Mexican player, won the men's singles gold medal at the 1968 Mexico City Olympics (demonstration event), highlighting his skill on home soil.

14. B. Margaret Court. Court won the women's singles gold medal at the 1968 Mexico City Olympics (demonstration event), adding to her impressive career achievements.
15. B. Four times. Tennis appeared as a full medal sport at the Olympics four times before 1970: 1896, 1900, 1904, and 1924.
16. A. John Pius Boland. Boland was the first player to win both singles and doubles gold medals at the same Olympics, achieving this at the 1896 Athens Games.
17. B. Great Britain. Great Britain won the most tennis medals at the Olympics before 1970, reflecting the country's strong tradition in the sport.
18. B. Clay. Tennis was played on clay courts at the 1924 Paris Olympics, which was a common surface for European tournaments.

Did You Know?

Tennis was an Olympic event seven times, beginning in 1896, before being removed for the next eight Olympic games.

CHAPTER 9:
INTERNATIONAL TENNIS FEDERATION

1. In which year was the International Tennis Federation (ITF) founded?

    A. 1903
    B. 1913
    C. 1923
    D. 1933

2. Who is generally recognized as the initiator and driving force behind the founding of the ITF?

    A. Dwight F. Davis
    B. Duane Williams
    C. William Renshaw
    D. René Lacoste

3. The ITF was originally known by what name?

    A. International Tennis Association
    B. World Tennis Federation
    C. International Lawn Tennis Federation
    D. Global Tennis Union

4. How many national associations were founding members of the ITF?

    A. Eight
    B. Ten
    C. 12
    D. 15

5. Where was the inaugural conference of the ITF held?

    A. London, England
    B. Paris, France
    C. New York, U.S.A.
    D. Melbourne, Australia

6. Which country was given the perpetual right to organize the World Grass Championships?

    A. United States
    B. France
    C. Australia
    D. Great Britain

7. Which major global event interrupted the early years of the ITF?

    A. World War I
    B. World War II

C. The Great Depression
D. The Cold War

8. In which year did the United States Lawn Tennis Association (USLTA) join the ITF?

    A. 1913
    B. 1923
    C. 1933
    D. 1943

9. The ITF is responsible for organizing which major team competitions?

    A. Davis Cup and Billie Jean King Cup
    B. Hopman Cup and Laver Cup
    C. ATP Cup and WTA Finals
    D. World Team Tennis and Fed Cup

10. Which of these was a founding member country of the ITF?

    A. Canada
    B. Norway
    C. Spain
    D. Japan

11. The ITF's headquarters are located in which city?

    A. Paris
    B. London
    C. New York
    D. Melbourne

12. The ITF partners with which organizations to govern professional tennis?

    A. ATP and WTA
    B. IOC and FIFA
    C. USTA and LTA
    D. ITA and ITTF

13. Which event led to the ITF changing from its original name to the International Tennis Federation?

    A. Introduction of hard courts
    B. Inclusion of wheelchair tennis
    C. Expansion to beach tennis
    D. Globalization of the sport

14. How many national associations were members of the ITF as of 2023?

    A. 156
    B. 183
    C. 207
    D. 211

15. The ITF was founded to maintain and enforce what aspect of tennis?

    A. Tournament schedules
    B. Player rankings
    C. Rules of the game
    D. Sponsorship deals

16. Which ITF competition is specifically for mixed teams?

    A. Davis Cup
    B. Billie Jean King Cup
    C. Hopman Cup
    D. Laver Cup

17. The ITF sanctions circuits for which age ranges?

    A. Juniors and seniors
    B. Professionals and amateurs
    C. College and high school
    D. Veterans and legends

18. The ITF's governance responsibilities include promoting the game and preserving its integrity through what programs?

    A. Marketing and advertising
    B. Coaching and training
    C. Anti-doping and anti-corruption
    D. Media and broadcasting

Chapter 9 Answers:

1. B. 1913. The ITF was founded on March 1, 1913, to govern the sport of tennis worldwide.
2. B. Duane Williams. Duane Williams, an American living in Switzerland, was recognized as the initiator and driving force behind the foundation of the ITF. Unfortunately, he died in the sinking of the *RMS Titanic*.
3. C. International Lawn Tennis Federation. The ITF was originally known as the International Lawn Tennis Federation (ILTF) until it was renamed in 1977.
4. C. 12. Twelve national associations were founding members of the ITF, including countries like France, Great Britain, and Germany.
5. B. Paris, France. The inaugural conference of the ITF was held in Paris, France, at the headquarters of the Union des Sociétés Françaises de Sports Athlétiques (USFSA).
6. D. Great Britain. Great Britain's Lawn Tennis Association (LTA) was given the perpetual right to organize the World Grass Championships, which led to some initial disagreements with the United States.
7. A. World War I. World War I interrupted the early years of the ITF, affecting international competitions and the development of the sport.
8. B. 1923. The USLTA joined the ITF in 1923 after initial disagreements were resolved.
9. A. Davis Cup and Billie Jean King Cup. The ITF is responsible for organizing major team competitions such as the Davis Cup for men and the Billie Jean King Cup for women.
10. C. Spain. Spain was one of the founding member countries of the ITF, along with others like France, Great Britain, and Germany.
11. B. London. The ITF's headquarters are located in London, England.
12. A. ATP and WTA. The ITF partners with the Association of Tennis Professionals (ATP) and the Women's Tennis Association (WTA) to govern professional tennis.
13. D. Globalization of the sport. The ITF changed its name from the International Lawn Tennis Federation to the International Tennis Federation in 1977 to reflect the global nature of the sport.
14. D. 211. As of 2023, the ITF had 211 national associations as members.
15. C. Rules of the game. The ITF was founded to maintain and enforce the rules of tennis, ensuring consistency and fairness in the sport.

16. C. Hopman Cup. The Hopman Cup is an ITF competition specifically for mixed teams, featuring both male and female players.
17. A. Juniors and seniors. The ITF sanctions circuits for various age ranges, including juniors and seniors, to promote tennis at all levels.
18. C. Anti-doping and anti-corruption. The ITF's governance responsibilities include promoting the game and preserving its integrity through anti-doping and anti-corruption programs.

Did You Know?

Duane Williams is credited with the founding of the ITF, which took place in March 1913, but Williams died in April 1912.

CHAPTER 10:
EARLY FEDERATION CUP

1. In which year was the Federation Cup (now known as the Billie Jean King Cup) founded?

    A. 1953
    B. 1963
    C. 1973
    D. 1983

2. Who was the driving force behind the creation of the Federation Cup?

    A. Billie Jean King
    B. Hazel Hotchkiss Wightman
    C. Nell Hopman
    D. Mary Hardwick Hare

3. The Federation Cup was launched to celebrate the anniversary of which organization?

    A. Women's Tennis Association (WTA)
    B. International Olympic Committee (IOC)
    C. International Tennis Federation (ITF)
    D. United States Tennis Association (USTA)

4. How many countries participated in the inaugural Federation Cup in 1963?

    A. Eight
    B. 12
    C. 16
    D. 20

5. Where was the first Federation Cup held?

    A. Wimbledon, England
    B. Roland Garros, France
    C. Queen's Club, England
    D. Melbourne Park, Australia

6. Which country won the first Federation Cup in 1963?

    A. Australia
    B. United States
    C. Great Britain
    D. France

7. The Federation Cup was renamed to the Fed Cup in which year?

    A. 1975
    B. 1985

C. 1995
   D. 2005

8. Who was the first female tennis player to win a match in the Federation Cup?

   A. Billie Jean King
   B. Margaret Court
   C. Darlene Hard
   D. Lesley Turner

9. The Federation Cup was initially played over how many days?

   A. Three
   B. Five
   C. Seven
   D. Ten

10. Which country dominated the Federation Cup in the early years, winning seven of the first 11 championships?

    A. United States
    B. Australia
    C. France
    D. Great Britain

11. The Federation Cup format changed in 1992 to include which new feature?

    A. Round-robin play
    B. Knockout rounds
    C. Group stages
    D. Home-and-away ties

12. Who won the Federation Cup in 1974, marking their seventh victory in the competition?

    A. Italy
    B. Spain
    C. Australia
    D. Germany

13. The Federation Cup was renamed to the Billie Jean King Cup in which year?

    A. 2010
    B. 2015

- C. 2020
- D. 2025

14. Which player holds the record for the most singles wins in Federation Cup history?

    A. Chris Evert
    B. Martina Navratilova
    C. Steffi Graf
    D. Billie Jean King

15. How many teams competed in the Federation Cup in 1970?

    A. 22
    B. 32
    C. 42
    D. 52

16. The Federation Cup was founded to promote what aspect of tennis?

    A. Professional tournaments
    B. Women's team competition
    C. Mixed doubles events
    D. Junior development

17. Which country won the Federation Cup in 1983, ending the United States' dominance?

    A. Australia
    B. Czechoslovakia
    C. France
    D. Germany

18. The Federation Cup is the women's equivalent of which men's tennis competition?

    A. Davis Cup
    B. Hopman Cup
    C. ATP Cup
    D. Laver Cup

Chapter 10 Answers:

1. B. 1963. The Federation Cup was founded in 1963.
2. D. Mary Hardwick Hare. Mary Hardwick Hare, a British resident of the United States, presented a dossier proving overwhelming support for a women's team tennis competition.
3. C. International Tennis Federation (ITF). The Federation Cup was launched to celebrate the 50th anniversary of the ITF.
4. C. 16. Sixteen countries participated in the inaugural Federation Cup in 1963, showcasing the global interest in women's team tennis.
5. C. Queen's Club, England. The first Federation Cup was held at Queen's Club in London, England.
6. B. United States. The United States won the first Federation Cup in 1963, defeating Australia in the final.
7. C. 1995. The Federation Cup was renamed the Fed Cup in 1995 to modernize the competition.
8. C. Darlene Hard. Darlene Hard, representing the United States, was the first female tennis player to win a match in the Federation Cup.
9. C. Seven. The Federation Cup was initially played over seven days, allowing for a comprehensive team competition.
10. B. Australia. Australia dominated the Federation Cup in the early years, winning seven of the first 11 championships.
11. D. Home-and-away ties. The Federation Cup format changed in 1992 to include home-and-away ties, making the competition more dynamic and engaging.
12. C. Australia. Australia won the Federation Cup in 1974, marking their seventh victory in the competition.
13. C. 2020. The Federation Cup was renamed to the Billie Jean King Cup in 2020 to honor the legendary tennis player and advocate for women's sports.
14. B. Martina Navratilova. Martina Navratilova holds the record for the most singles wins in Federation Cup history, showcasing her dominance in the competition.
15. A. 22. By 1970, 22 teams were competing in the Federation Cup, reflecting the growing popularity of the event.
16. B. Women's team competition. The Federation Cup was founded to promote women's team competition in tennis, providing a platform for female athletes to represent their countries.

17. B. Czechoslovakia. Czechoslovakia won the Federation Cup in 1983, stopping the United States from winning the tournament for an eighth straight time.
18. A. Davis Cup. The Federation Cup is the women's equivalent of the Davis Cup, which is the premier international team competition in men's tennis.

Did You Know?

Hazel Hotchkiss Wightman had the idea for a women's team competition in 1919, and she insisted on presenting a trophy at the 1923 annual contest between the USA and Great Britain.

CHAPTER 11:
EARLY PROFESSIONAL TOURS

1. In which year was the first professional tour organized?

    A. 1916
    B. 1926
    C. 1936
    D. 1946

2. Who was the promoter behind the first professional tennis tour?

    A. Dwight F. Davis
    B. C.C. Pyle
    C. Jack Kramer
    D. Bill Tilden

3. Which two players were the main attractions of the first professional tennis tour?

    A. Bill Tilden and Fred Perry
    B. Suzanne Lenglen and Vinnie Richards
    C. Henri Cochet and René Lacoste
    D. Ellsworth Vines and Don Budge

4. The first professional tennis tour primarily featured matches in which format?

    A. Round-robin
    B. Knockout
    C. Head-to-head
    D. Team competition

5. Which country hosted the majority of the matches in the first professional tennis tour?

    A. France
    B. Australia
    C. United States
    D. Great Britain

6. Who won the most matches in the first professional tennis tour?

    A. Suzanne Lenglen
    B. Vinnie Richards
    C. Bill Tilden
    D. Ellsworth Vines

7. The professional tennis tours were interrupted by which major global event?

    A. World War I
    B. World War II
    C. The Great Depression
    D. The Cold War

8. In which year did the professional tennis tours resume after being interrupted by a major global event?

    A. 1946
    B. 1950
    C. 1954
    D. 1958

9. Which player dominated the professional tennis tours in the late 1940s and early 1950s?

    A. Jack Kramer
    B. Pancho González
    C. Ken Rosewall
    D. Rod Laver

10. The professional tennis tours led to the creation of which major tennis event in 1968?

    A. Wimbledon
    B. Davis Cup
    C. Open Era
    D. ATP Tour

11. Who was the first player to win a "Professional Grand Slam" by winning the major professional tournaments in a single year?

    A. Bill Tilden
    B. Ellsworth Vines
    C. Jack Kramer
    D. Ken Rosewall

12. The professional tennis courts were known for featuring matches on which type of court surface?

    A. Grass
    B. Clay
    C. Hard
    D. Wood

13. Which tournament was considered the most prestigious professional event before the Open Era?

- A. U.S. Pro Tennis Championships
- B. French Pro Championship
- C. Wembley Championship
- D. Australian Pro Championship

14. Who was the first player to turn professional after winning a major amateur title?

    - A. Fred Perry
    - B. Don Budge
    - C. Rod Laver
    - D. Tony Trabert

15. The professional tennis tours often included matches in which format?

    - A. Singles only
    - B. Doubles only
    - C. Singles and doubles
    - D. Mixed doubles

16. Which player was known for his powerful serve and domination of the professional tours of the 1950s?

    - A. Jack Kramer
    - B. Pancho González
    - C. Ken Rosewall
    - D. Lew Hoad

17. The professional tennis tours were instrumental in the formation of which organization in 1977?

    - A. ITF
    - B. WTA
    - C. ATP
    - D. USTA

18. The professional tennis tours were initially organized to provide which of these for the players?

    - A. Sponsorship deals
    - B. Prize money
    - C. Travel expenses
    - D. Coaching opportunities

Chapter 11 Answers:

1. B. 1926. The first professional tennis tour was organized in 1926 by promoter C. C. Pyle, presenting exhibition matches to paying audiences.
2. B. C. C. Pyle. C. C. Pyle was the promoter behind the first professional tennis tour, which included American and French players.
3. B. Suzanne Lenglen and Vinnie Richards. Suzanne Lenglen and Vinnie Richards were the main attractions of the first professional tennis tour, drawing large crowds.
4. C. Head-to-head. The first professional tennis tour primarily featured head-to-head matches, a format that was popular for its competitive nature.
5. C. United States. The majority of the matches in the first professional tennis tour were hosted in the United States, reflecting the country's growing interest in tennis.
6. B. Vinnie Richards. Vinnie Richards won the most matches in the first professional tennis tour, showcasing his skill and popularity.
7. B. World War II. The professional tennis tours were interrupted by World War II, affecting international sports events.
8. A. 1946. The professional tennis tours resumed in 1946 after World War II, with an increasing number of prominent professional players.
9. A. Jack Kramer. Jack Kramer, known for his powerful serve and strategic play, dominated the professional tennis tours in the late 1940s and early 1950s.
10. C. Open Era. The professional tennis tours led to the creation of the Open Era in 1968, allowing both amateurs and professionals to compete in major tournaments.
11. D. Ken Rosewall. Ken Rosewall was the first player to win a "Professional Grand Slam" by winning the major professional tournaments in a single year.
12. D. Wood. The professional tennis tours were known for featuring matches on wood courts, which were common for indoor events.
13. A. U.S. Pro Tennis Championships. The U.S. Pro Tennis Championships was considered the most prestigious professional event before the Open Era.
14. B. Don Budge. Don Budge was the first player to turn professional after winning a major amateur title, transitioning to the professional tours in 1938.

15. C. Singles and doubles. The professional tennis tours often included matches in both singles and doubles formats, providing varied competition.
16. B. Pancho González. Pancho González was known for his powerful serve and dominated the professional tours in the 1950s.
17. C. ATP. The professional tennis tours were instrumental in the formation of the Association of Tennis Professionals (ATP) in 1972, which governs men's professional tennis.
18. B. Prize money. The professional tennis tours were initially organized to provide prize money for players, allowing them to earn a living from the sport.

Did You Know?

The Bristol Cup is considered one of the first major professional tennis tournaments, beginning back in 1920.

CHAPTER 12:
THE 1900S

1. In which year did the first women's doubles tournament take place at Wimbledon?

    A. 1900
    B. 1902
    C. 1906
    D. 1913

2. Who was the first player to win the men's singles title at Wimbledon three times in the 20th century?

    A. William Renshaw
    B. Laurence Doherty
    C. Norman Brookes
    D. Anthony Wilding

3. The first U.S. National Championships mixed doubles event was held in which year?

    A. 1900
    B. 1902
    C. 1905
    D. 1907

4. How many players participated in the first women's singles tournament at the U.S. National Championships in 1900?

    A. Four
    B. Six
    C. Eight
    D. Ten

5. Which surface was used for the French Open during the early 1900s?

    A. Grass
    B. Clay
    C. Sand
    D. Hard

6. Who was the first female tennis player to win the women's singles title at Wimbledon and the U.S. National Championships in the same year?

    A. Charlotte Cooper Sterry
    B. Dorothea Lambert Chambers
    C. May Sutton
    D. Blanche Bingley Hillyard

7. Tennis was included in the Olympics for the second time in which year?

   A. 1900
   B. 1904
   C. 1908
   D. 1912

8. Who was the Australian Open men's singles champion of 1909?

   A. J.P. Keane
   B. Ernie Parker
   C. Tom Crooks
   D. Anthony Wilding

9. Who won the men's singles title at the U.S. National Championships (now the U.S. Open) in 1906, marking his first victory in the tournament?

   A. William Larned
   B. Holcombe Ward
   C. Beals Wright
   D. Fred Alexander

10. Which country won the Davis Cup in 1905, marking their second victory in the competition?

    A. United States
    B. Great Britain
    C. Australia
    D. France

11. Who was the first player to win the men's singles title at Wimbledon and the Australian Open in the same year?

    A. Bill Tilden
    B. Fred Perry
    C. Tony Wilding
    D. Norman Brookes

12. May Sutton won her first and only women's singles title at the U.S. National Championships in which year?

    A. 1900
    B. 1902
    C. 1904
    D. 1906

13. Which player won the men's singles title at Wimbledon in 1908, marking his second victory in the tournament?

    A. Norman Brookes
    B. Anthony Wilding
    C. Laurence Doherty
    D. William Renshaw

14. Who won the women's singles title at the French Open in 1909?

    A. Jeanne Matthey
    B. Adine Masson
    C. Marguerite Broquedis
    D. Comtesse de Kermel

15. How many times did Laurence Doherty win the men's singles title at Wimbledon in the early 1900s?

    A. Two
    B. Three
    C. Four
    D. Five

16. Who won the men's singles title at the first U.S. National Championships of the 20th century?

    A. Malcolm Whitman
    B. Dwight Davis
    C. J. Parmly Paret
    D. William Larned

17. Which player won the men's singles title at the French Open in 1907, which would end up being his third of eight titles?

    A. André Gobert
    B. Max Décugis
    C. Michel Vacherot
    D. André Vacherot

18. Who won the women's singles championship at Wimbledon in 1900?

    A. Blanche Hillyard
    B. Charlotte Cooper Sterry
    C. Agnes Morton
    D. Louisa Martin

Chapter 12 Answers:

1. D. 1913. The first women's doubles tournament at Wimbledon took place in 1913, expanding the competition for female players.
2. B. Laurence Doherty. Laurence Doherty was the first player to win the men's singles title at Wimbledon three times in the 20th century, achieving this feat in 1902, 1903, and 1904.
3. C. 1905. The first U.S. National Championships mixed doubles event was held in 1905, providing a new format for competition.
4. A. Four. Four players participated in the first women's singles tournament at the U.S. National Championships in 1900, reflecting the early stages of women's participation.
5. C. Sand. The French Open was played on sand courts during the early 1900s, before switching to clay.
6. C. May Sutton. May Sutton was the first female tennis player to win the women's singles title at Wimbledon and the U.S. National Championships in the same year, achieving this in 1905.
7. C. 1908. Tennis was included in the Olympics for the second time in 1908, held in London.
8. D. Anthony Wildling. Wildling defeated Ernie Parker in straight sets to capture his second title.
9. C. Beals Wright. Wright won the men's singles title at the U.S. National Championships in 1906, marking his first victory in the tournament.
10. B. Great Britain. Great Britain won the Davis Cup in 1905, marking their second victory in the competition.
11. D. Norman Brookes. Brookes was the first player to win the men's singles title at Wimbledon and the Australian Open in the same year, achieving this in 1907.
12. C. 1904. She was also the first American woman to win the singles title at Wimbledon.
13. B. Anthony Wilding. Wilding won the men's singles title at Wimbledon in 1908, marking his second victory in the tournament.
14. A. Jeanne Matthey. Matthey won her first of four straight titles in 1909.
15. D. Five times. Laurence Doherty won the men's singles title at Wimbledon five times in the early 1900s, from 1902 to 1906.
16. A. Malcolm Whitman. It was his third straight and final U.S. National Championships crown in men's singles. He would go on to have some success in Davis Cup competitions.

17. B. Max Décugis. Décugis won the men's singles title at the French Open in 1909, marking his first victory in the tournament.
18. A. Blanche Hillyard. It was her sixth and final singles title at Wimbledon.

Did You Know?

Despite his successful tennis career, Tony Wilding died at the age of 31, quite young considering his athletic prowess.

CHAPTER 13:
THE 1910S

1. In which year did the U.S. National Championships move to the West Side Tennis Club in Forest Hills, New York?

    A. 1910
    B. 1915
    C. 1917
    D. 1919

2. Who won the men's singles title at Wimbledon in 1910, marking his first victory in the tournament?

    A. Anthony Wilding
    B. Norman Brookes
    C. Arthur Gore
    D. Bill Tilden

3. Which of these women won the singles tournament at the 1910 U.S. National Championships?

    A. Hazel Hotchkiss Wightman
    B. Evelyn Sears
    C. Helen Homans
    D. Mary Browne

4. How many players participated in the men's singles tournament at the 1910 U.S. National Championships?

    A. 32
    B. 64
    C. 128
    D. 256

5. Which surface was used for the Wimbledon Championships during the early 1910s?

    A. Grass
    B. Clay
    C. Hard
    D. Carpet

6. Who was the winner of the women's singles title at Wimbledon in 1913?

    A. Charlotte Cooper Sterry
    B. Dorothea Lambert Chambers
    C. May Sutton
    D. Ethel Larcombe

7. Tennis was included in the Olympics for the third time in which year?

    A. 1912
    B. 1916
    C. 1920
    D. 1924

8. Which of these players won the French Open men's singles championship in 1910?

    A. Maurice Germot
    B. André Gobert
    C. Max Décugis
    D. Georges Gault

9. Who won the men's singles title at the U.S. National Championships in 1915, marking his first victory at the tournament?

    A. William Johnston
    B. Maurice McLoughlin
    C. Bill Tilden
    D. Richard Norris Williams

10. Which country won the Davis Cup in 1913, marking their third victory in the competition?

    A. United States
    B. Great Britain
    C. Australia
    D. France

11. Who was the first player to win the men's singles title at Wimbledon and the U.S. National Championships in the same year during the 1910s?

    A. Bill Tilden
    B. Fred Perry
    C. Tony Wilding
    D. William Johnston

12. How many different women won the singles title at the French Open during the 1910s?

    A. Two
    B. Three
    C. Four
    D. Five

13. Which player won the men's singles title at Wimbledon in 1914, marking his second victory at the tournament?

    A. Norman Brookes
    B. Anthony Wilding
    C. Laurence Doherty
    D. William Renshaw

14. Which female tennis player won the singles title at the U.S. National Championships in 1915?

    A. Hazel Hotchkiss Wightman
    B. Molla Bjurstedt Mallory
    C. Mary Browne
    D. Helen Wills

15. How many times did Anthony Wilding win the men's singles title at Wimbledon in the early 1910s?

    A. Two
    B. Three
    C. Four
    D. Five

16. William Larned's victory at the 1910 U.S. National Championships was which of his career titles at the event?

    A. Fourth
    B. Fifth
    C. Sixth
    D. Seventh

17. Which player won the men's singles title at the French Open in 1912, marking his first victory in the tournament?

    A. Paul Ayme
    B. Max Décugis
    C. André Gobert
    D. William Laurentz

18. Which of these women finished as the runner-up at the 1912 French Open women's singles tournament?

    A. Marie Danet
    B. Jeanne Matthey
    C. Suzanne Lengler
    D. Germaine Regnier

Chapter 13 Answers:

1. B. 1915. The U.S. National Championships moved to the West Side Tennis Club in Forest Hills, New York, in 1915, providing a new venue for the prestigious tournament.
2. A. Anthony Wilding. Wilding won the men's singles title at Wimbledon in 1910, marking his first victory in the tournament and beginning his dominance in the early 1910s.
3. A. Hazel Hotchkiss Wightman. Hotchkiss Wightman won her second consecutive singles title in 1910, and she added a third one a year later.
4. B. 64. Sixty-four players participated in the men's singles tournament at the 1910 U.S. National Championships, reflecting the growing popularity of the event.
5. A. Grass. The Wimbledon Championships were played on grass courts during the early 1910s, maintaining the traditional surface for the tournament.
6. B. Dorothea Lambert Chambers. She won her sixth of seven titles in 1913, and she won her final title one year later, just before World War I canceled further competition until 1919.
7. A. 1912. Tennis was included in the Olympics for the third time in 1912, held in Stockholm.
8. A. Maurice Germot. He won his third and final French Open title in 1910, falling to André Gobert in the final the next year.
9. A. William Johnston. Johnston won the men's singles title at the U.S. National Championships in 1915, marking his first victory in the tournament.
10. B. Great Britain. Great Britain won the Davis Cup in 1913, marking their third victory in the competition.
11. D. William Johnston. Johnston was the first player to win the men's singles title at Wimbledon and the U.S. National Championships in the same year during the 1910s.
12. A. Two. Jeanne Matthey and Marguerite Broquedis split the five championships of the decade between them, as the other tournaments were canceled by World War I.
13. B. Anthony Wilding. Wilding won the men's singles title at Wimbledon in 1914, marking his second victory in the tournament.
14. B. Molla Bjurstedt Mallory. Mallory was the first female tennis player to win the women's singles title at the U.S. National Championships in 1915.

15. C. Four times. Anthony Wilding won the men's singles title at Wimbledon four times in the early 1910s, from 1910 to 1913.
16. C. Six. It was his sixth win, and it was the fourth consecutive win. He would win his final title the next year.
17. C. André Gobert. Gobert won the men's singles title at the French Open in 1912, marking his first victory in the tournament.
18. A. Marie Danet. She lost to Jeanne Matthey, who successfully won her fourth straight French Open title.

Did You Know?

André Gobert never won a Grand Slam, but he reached number three in the rankings back in 1919.

CHAPTER 14:
THE 1920S

1. In which year did Suzanne Lenglen win her first Wimbledon singles title?

    A. 1920
    B. 1922
    C. 1924
    D. 1926

2. Who won the men's singles title at the U.S. National Championships in 1920, which was his first time winning the tournament?

    A. Bill Tilden
    B. William Johnston
    C. Richard Norris Williams
    D. Maurice McLoughlin

3. Which of these women won the first four French Open singles championships of the 1920s?

    A. Germaine Golding
    B. Marguerite Broquedis
    C. Suzanne Lenglen
    D. Julie Vlasto

4. How many players participated in the men's singles tournament at the 1920 Wimbledon Championships?

    A. 64
    B. 128
    C. 256
    D. 512

5. Which surface was used for the U.S. National Championships during the 1920s?

    A. Grass
    B. Clay
    C. Hard
    D. Carpet

6. Who was the first female player to win the singles title at Wimbledon and the French Open in the same year?

    A. Suzanne Lenglen
    B. Helen Wills
    C. Kitty McKane
    D. Elizabeth Ryan

7. Tennis was included in the Olympics for the fourth time in which year?

    A. 1920
    B. 1924
    C. 1928
    D. 1932

8. Who won the men's singles title at the Australian Open in 1920?

    A. Pat O'Hara Wood
    B. James Anderson
    C. John Hawkes
    D. Rice Gemmell

9. Who won the men's singles title at Wimbledon in 1927, marking his first victory at the fabled event?

    A. René Lacoste
    B. Henri Cochet
    C. Jean Borotra
    D. Bill Tilden

10. Which country won the Davis Cup in 1923, which was their fourth championship in the event?

    A. United States
    B. Great Britain
    C. Australia
    D. France

11. Who was the first player to win the men's singles title at Wimbledon and the U.S. National Championships in the same year during the 1920s?

    A. Bill Tilden
    B. Fred Perry
    C. Tony Wilding
    D. René Lacoste

12. Which of these women won the Australian Open for the first time in 1922?

    A. Esna Boyd
    B. Margaret Molesworth
    C. Sylvia Lance Harper
    D. Daphne Akhurst

13. Which player won the men's singles title at the French Open in 1925, which was his first time winning the tournament?

    A. René Lacoste
    B. Henri Cochet
    C. Jean Borotra
    D. Bill Tilden

14. Which of these women won the singles title at the U.S. National Championships in 1923?

    A. Helen Wills
    B. Molla Bjurstedt Mallory
    C. Suzanne Lenglen
    D. Kitty McKane

15. How many times did Bill Tilden win the men's singles title at the U.S. National Championships during the 1920s?

    A. Four
    B. Five
    C. Six
    D. Seven

16. Which of these men won the singles title at the Australasian Championships in 1926?

    A. John Hawkes
    B. Richard Schlesinger
    C. James Anderson
    D. Bert St. John

17. Which player won the men's singles title at Wimbledon in 1929, which was his second victory at that tournament?

    A. Bill Tilden
    B. Henri Cochet
    C. Sidney Wood
    D. Wilmer Allison

18. Esna Boyd finally won the women's singles title at the 1927 Australasian Championships after finishing runner-up for how many years in a row?

    A. Two
    B. Three
    C. Four
    D. Five

Chapter 14 Answers:

1. A. 1920. Suzanne Lenglen achieved her first Wimbledon singles title in 1920, beginning her dominance in women's tennis.
2. A. Bill Tilden. Tilden won the men's singles title at the U.S. National Championships in 1920, marking his first victory in the tournament.
3. C. Suzanne Lenglen. She defeated Broquedis in the final once, then defeated Germaine Golding three times in the final to win the four titles.
4. B. 128. One hundred twenty-eight players participated in the men's singles tournament at the 1920 Wimbledon Championships, reflecting the event's growing popularity.
5. A. Grass. The U.S. National Championships were played on grass courts during the 1920s, maintaining the traditional surface for the tournament.
6. A. Suzanne Lenglen. Lenglen was the first female tennis player to win the women's singles title at Wimbledon and the French Open in the same year, achieving this in 1920.
7. B. 1924. Tennis was included in the Olympics for the fourth time in 1924, held in Paris.
8. A. Pat O'Hara Wood. He defeated Ronald Thomas in the final, needing five sets to finish the match.
9. A. René Lacoste. Lacoste won the men's singles title at Wimbledon in 1927, marking his first victory in the tournament.
10. A. United States. The United States won the Davis Cup in 1923, marking their fourth victory in the competition.
11. A. Bill Tilden. Tilden was the first player to win the men's singles title at Wimbledon and the U.S. National Championships in the same year during the 1920s.
12. B. Margaret Molesworth. She won the first two Australasian Championships in 1922 and 1923.
13. A. René Lacoste. Lacoste won the men's singles title at the French Open in 1925, marking his first victory in the tournament.
14. A. Helen Wills. Wills was the first female tennis player to win the women's singles title at the U.S. National Championships in 1923.
15. D. Seven times. Bill Tilden won the men's singles title at the U.S. National Championships seven times in the 1920s, from 1920 to 1925, and one more in 1929.
16. A. John Hawkes. It was the first and only singles title for Hawkes at the Australian Open/Australasian Championships.

17. B. Henri Cochet. Cochet won the men's singles title at Wimbledon in 1929, after winning it for the first time in 1927.
18. D. Five. Boyd had been the runner-up in every iteration of the tournament until she finally broke through in 1927.

Did You Know?

Bill Tilden won the U.S. Open six times in a row, then one more time in 1929 for a total of seven wins in the 1920s.

CHAPTER 15:
THE 1930S

1. In which year did the first professional tennis tour featuring Don Budge take place?

    A. 1930
    B. 1933
    C. 1936
    D. 1939

2. Who won the men's singles title at Wimbledon in 1930, which was his third and final victory at that event?

    A. Bill Tilden
    B. Fred Perry
    C. Henri Cochet
    D. Jack Crawford

3. Which of these women won the singles title at the U.S. National Championships in 1930?

    A. Betty Nuthall
    B. Helen Willis Moody
    C. Helen Jacobs
    D. Alice Marble

4. How many players participated in the men's singles tournament at the 1930 French Open?

    A. 64
    B. 128
    C. 256
    D. 512

5. Which surface was used for the Australian Open during the 1930s?

    A. Grass
    B. Clay
    C. Hard
    D. Carpet

6. Who won the women's singles title at Wimbledon in 1934?

    A. Helen Willis Moody
    B. Dorothy Round
    C. Alice Marble
    D. Simonne Mathieu

7. Tennis was included in the Olympics for the fifth time in what year?

A. 1932
   B. 1936
   C. 1940
   D. 1944

8. Who won the men's singles title at the 1930 French Open?

   A. Henri Cochet
   B. Gottfried von Cramm
   C. Fred Perry
   D. Don Budge

9. Who won the men's singles title at the U.S. National Championships in 1937, marking his first of two career titles at the event?

   A. Fred Perry
   B. Don Budge
   C. Jack Crawford
   D. Wilmer Allison

10. Which country won the Davis Cup in 1933, which was their sixth title?

    A. United States
    B. Great Britain
    C. Australia
    D. France

11. Who was the first player to win the men's singles title at Wimbledon and the French Open in the same year during the 1930s?

    A. Bill Tilden
    B. Fred Perry
    C. Tony Wilding
    D. Henri Cochet

12. During which year did Daphne Akhurst win her final singles title at the Australian Championships?

    A. 1930
    B. 1932
    C. 1933
    D. 1935

13. Which player won the men's singles title at Wimbledon in 1934, marking his first of three career victories at the tournament?

A. Fred Perry
   B. Don Budge
   C. Jack Crawford
   D. Ellsworth Vines

14. Who was the champion of the women's singles at the U.S. National Championships in 1933?

   A. Helen Wills Moody
   B. Alice Marble
   C. Dorothy Round
   D. Simonne Mathieu

15. How many times did Fred Perry win the men's singles title at Wimbledon in the 1930s?

   A. Two
   B. Three
   C. Four
   D. Five

16. Jack Crawford won his only French Open title in what year?

   A. 1933
   B. 1935
   C. 1937
   D. 1939

17. Which of these players won the men's singles title at the Australian Open in 1936, his first of three victories at the event?

   A. Jack Crawford
   B. Don Budge
   C. Adrian Quist
   D. John Bromwich

18. How many times did Helen Moody win the women's singles title at Wimbledon during the 1930s?

   A. Two
   B. Three
   C. Four
   D. Five

Chapter 15 Answers:

1. D. 1939. The first professional tennis tour featuring Don Budge took place in 1939, showcasing his talent and drawing large crowds.
2. C. Henri Cochet. Cochet won the men's singles title at Wimbledon in 1930, marking his first victory in the tournament.
3. A. Betty Nuthall. It was the only time Nuthall won the singles title at the U.S. National Championships.
4. B. 128. One hundred twenty-eight players participated in the men's singles tournament at the 1930 French Open, reflecting the event's growing popularity.
5. A. Grass. The Australian Open was played on grass courts during the 1930s, maintaining the traditional surface for the tournament.
6. B. Dorothy Round. It was her first championship at Wimbledon, and she would get one more just a few years later.
7. B. 1936. Tennis was included in the Olympics for the fifth time in 1936, held in Berlin.
8. A. Henri Cochet. Cochet won his fourth of five French Open titles at the 1930 French Open.
9. B. Don Budge. Budge would also win the title in 1938, defeating Gene Mako in four sets.
10. A. United States. The United States won the Davis Cup in 1933, marking their fifth victory in the competition.
11. B. Fred Perry. Perry was the first player to win the men's singles title at Wimbledon and the French Open in the same year during the 1930s.
12. A. 1930. Daphne Akhurst was crowned the first women's singles champion at the Australian Open in the 1930s.
13. A. Fred Perry. Perry won the men's singles title at Wimbledon in 1934, marking his first victory in the tournament.
14. B. Alice Marble. Marble was the first female tennis player to win the women's singles title at the U.S. National Championships in 1933.
15. B. Three times. Fred Perry won the men's singles title at Wimbledon three times in the 1930s, from 1934 to 1936.
16. A. 1933. Crawford defeated Henri Cochet in the final, denying him a sixth French Open title.
17. C. Adrian Quist. Quist defeated Jack Crawford in a five-set match to win the title.
18. D. Five times. She won the event in 1930, 1932, 1933, 1935, and 1938. She never finished as the runner-up during that period.

Did You Know?

Don Budge completed the Grand Slam in 1938, but he also won Wimbledon and the U.S. Open in 1937.

CHAPTER 16:
THE 1940S

1. In which year did Wimbledon begin operating again after the end of World War II?

    A. 1944
    B. 1945
    C. 1946
    D. 1947

2. Who won the men's singles title at Wimbledon in 1947, which was his first time winning the tournament?

    A. Jack Kramer
    B. Ted Schroeder
    C. Yvon Petra
    D. Frank Parker

3. Which of these women won the U.S. National Championships in 1940?

    A. Alice Marble
    B. Sarah Palfrey Cooke
    C. Pauline Betz
    D. Louise Brough

4. How many players participated in the men's singles tournament at the 1946 Wimbledon Championships?

    A. 64
    B. 128
    C. 256
    D. 512

5. Which surface was used for the French Open during the 1940s?

    A. Grass
    B. Clay
    C. Hard
    D. Carpet

6. Who won the women's singles title at Wimbledon in 1946?

    A. Pauline Betz
    B. Margaret Osborne duPont
    C. Louise Brough
    D. Doris Hart

7. Tennis was included in the Olympics for the sixth time in which year?

A. 1940
B. 1944
C. 1948
D. 1952

8. Which of these men won the Australian Open in 1940?

    A. Adrian Quist
    B. Jack Crawford
    C. Dinny Pails
    D. John Bromwich

9. Who won the men's singles title at the U.S. National Championships in 1948, which was his first victory in the tournament?

    A. Jack Kramer
    B. Ted Schroeder
    C. Frank Parker
    D. Pancho González

10. Which country won the Davis Cup in 1946, which was their sixth trophy in the tournament?

    A. United States
    B. Great Britain
    C. Australia
    D. France

11. Who was the first player to win the men's singles title at Wimbledon and U.S. National Championships in the same year during the 1940s?

    A. Jack Kramer
    B. Fred Perry
    C. Tony Wilding
    D. Bill Tilden

12. Which of these players won the Australian Open in 1940?

    A. Nancye Wynne Bolton
    B. Joyce Fitch
    C. Doris Hart
    D. Louise Brough

13. Which player won the men's singles title at the French Open in 1946, which was his first and only victory at the tournament?

    A. Marcel Bernard
    B. Henri Cochet

- C. Jean Borotra
- D. Bill Tilden

14. Who won the women's singles title at the U.S. National Championships in 1947?

    - A. Pauline Betz
    - B. Margaret Osborne
    - C. Louise Brough
    - D. Doris Hart

15. How many times did Jack Kramer win the men's singles title at Wimbledon during the 1940s?

    - A. One
    - B. Two
    - C. Three
    - D. Four

16. Which of these men won the Australian Open in 1940?

    - A. Adrian Quist
    - B. Ted Schroeder
    - C. Jack Kramer
    - D. Marcel Bernard

17. Which player won the men's singles title at Wimbledon in 1949, capturing his first title at the tournament?

    - A. Jack Kramer
    - B. Ted Schroeder
    - C. Yvon Petra
    - D. Frank Parker

18. Which of these women won the singles title at Wimbledon in 1946?

    - A. Kay Stammers
    - B. Louise Brough
    - C. Pauline Betz
    - D. Shirley Fry

Chapter 16 Answers:

1. C. 1946. Wimbledon resumed after World War II in 1946, despite the damage to Centre Court from bombing.
2. A. Jack Kramer. Kramer won the men's singles title at Wimbledon in 1947, his first and only win at the tournament.
3. A. Alice Marble. It was her fourth and final title at the tournament. It was also her third in a row.
4. B. 128. One hundred twenty-eight players participated in the men's singles tournament at the 1946 Wimbledon Championships, reflecting the event's return to prominence.
5. B. Clay. The French Open was played on clay courts during the 1940s, maintaining the traditional surface for the tournament.
6. A. Pauline Betz. Betz was the first female tennis player to win the women's singles title at Wimbledon in 1946.
7. C. 1948. Tennis was included in the Olympics for the sixth time in 1948, held in London.
8. A. Adrian Quist. He defeated Jack Crawford in the final to win his second Australian Open, the last one before World War II interrupted play for the next five years.
9. A. Jack Kramer. Kramer won the men's singles title at the U.S. National Championships in 1948, marking his first victory in the tournament.
10. A. United States. The United States won the Davis Cup in 1946, marking their sixth victory in the competition.
11. A. Jack Kramer. Kramer was the first player to win the men's singles title at Wimbledon and the U.S. National Championships in the same year during the 1940s.
12. A. Nancye Wynne Bolton. She was crowned champion in 1940 after she defeated Thelma Coyne Long in three sets.
13. A. Marcel Bernard. Bernard won the men's singles title at the French Open in 1946, marking his first victory in the tournament.
14. B. Margaret Osborne duPont. Osborne duPont was the first female tennis player to win the women's singles title at the U.S. National Championships in 1947.
15. B. Two. Jack Kramer won the men's singles title at Wimbledon twice in the 1940s, in 1947 and 1948.
16. A. Adrian Quist. It was his second title at the Australian Open, though he would collect one more in 1948.

17. B. Ted Schroeder. Schroeder won the men's singles title at Wimbledon in 1949, marking his first victory in the tournament.
18. C. Pauline Betz. It was her only championship at the tournament, and the only time she reached the final.

Did You Know?

Pauline Betz won Wimbledon and the U.S. Open in 1946, earning her the top ranking for women players during that year.

CHAPTER 17: THE 1950S

1. In which year did Maureen Connolly win her first Grand Slam event?

   A. 1950
   B. 1951
   C. 1952
   D. 1953

2. Who won the men's singles title at Wimbledon in 1950, which was his first victory in the tournament?

   A. Jack Kramer
   B. Frank Sedgman
   C. Budge Patty
   D. Lew Hoad

3. Which of these women won the singles title at the U.S. National Championships in 1950?

   A. Margaret Osborne
   B. Maureen Connolly
   C. Doris Hart
   D. Shirley Fry

4. How many players participated in the men's singles tournament at the 1950 French Open?

   A. 64
   B. 128
   C. 256
   D. 512

5. Which surface was used for the Australian Open during the 1950s?

   A. Grass
   B. Clay
   C. Hard
   D. Carpet

6. Which of these players won the women's singles title at Wimbledon in 1951?

   A. Maureen Connolly
   B. Doris Hart
   C. Louise Brough
   D. Shirley Fry

7. Who won the men's singles title at the U.S. Pro Tennis Championships in 1959?

    A. Pancho González
    B. Ken Rosewall
    C. Tony Trabert
    D. Lew Hoad

8. Which of these men won the singles title at the French Open in 1950?

    A. Sven Davidson
    B. Eric Sturgess
    C. Jaroslav Drobny
    D. Budge Patty

9. Who won the men's singles title at the U.S. National Championships in 1955, which was his second and final win at the event?

    A. Ken Rosewall
    B. Lew Hoad
    C. Pancho González
    D. Tony Trabert

10. Which country won the Davis Cup in 1953, which was their seventh time winning the tournament?

    A. United States
    B. Great Britain
    C. Australia
    D. France

11. Which of these players was the first in the 1950s to win Wimbledon and U.S. National Championships in the same year?

    A. Jack Kramer
    B. Frank Sedgman
    C. Tony Trabert
    D. Lew Hoad

12. Which of these women won the Australian Open in 1950?

    A. Nancye Wynne Bolton
    B. Maureen Connolly
    C. Doris Hart
    D. Louise Brough

13. Which of these players won their first Wimbledon singles title in 1956?

    A. Lew Hoad
    B. Ken Rosewall
    C. Frank Sedgman
    D. Tony Trabert

14. Who won the women's singles title at the U.S. National Championships in 1953?

    A. Maureen Connolly
    B. Doris Hart
    C. Louise Brough
    D. Shirley Fry

15. How many times did Lew Hoad win the men's singles title at Wimbledon during the 1950s?

    A. One
    B. Two
    C. Three
    D. Four

16. Ken Rosewall won the men's singles title at the 1953 French Open. How many years did it take him to win it a second time?

    A. Four
    B. 11
    C. 15
    D. 19

17. Which of these players won their first Australian Open in 1957?

    A. Ashley Cooper
    B. Neale Fraser
    C. Roy Emerson
    D. Ken Rosewall

18. Who won the 1956 women's singles title at the French Open?

    A. Angela Mortimer
    B. Dorothy Head Knode
    C. Althea Gibson
    D. Shirley Bloomer

Chapter 17 Answers:

1. B. 1951. Maureen Connolly achieved her first Grand Slam title in 1951, winning the U.S. National Championships.
2. C. Budge Patty. Patty won the men's singles title at Wimbledon in 1950, marking his first victory in the tournament.
3. A. Margaret Osborne. She won her third and final title at the event in 1950, defeating Doris Hart in the final.
4. B. 128. One hundred twenty-eight players participated in the men's singles tournament at the 1950 French Open.
5. A. Grass. The Australian Open was played on grass courts during the 1950s, maintaining the traditional surface for the tournament.
6. B. Doris Hart. Hart won the women's singles title at Wimbledon in 1951.
7. A. Pancho González. González won the men's singles title at the U.S. Pro Tennis Championships in 1959, marking his dominance in professional tennis. His victory was part of an impressive career where he was considered one of the best players of his era.
8. D. Budge Patty. He defeated Jaroslav Drobny of Egypt in five sets, capturing his first and only title at that tournament.
9. D. Tony Trabert. Trabert won the men's singles title at the U.S. National Championships in 1955, marking his first victory in the tournament.
10. C. Australia. Australia won the Davis Cup in 1953, marking their seventh victory in the competition.
11. C. Tony Trabert. Trabert was the first player to win the men's singles title at Wimbledon and the U.S. National Championships in the same year during the 1950s.
12. D. Louise Brough. She was part of the first all-American final at the Australian Open, defeating Doris Hart in three sets.
13. A. Lew Hoad. Hoad won the men's singles title at Wimbledon in 1956, marking his first victory in the tournament.
14. A. Maureen Connolly. Connolly won her third and final U.S. National Championships title in 1953.
15. B. Two. Lew Hoad won the men's singles title at Wimbledon twice in the 1950s, in 1956 and 1957.
16. C. 15. Rosewall did not win the French Open again until 1968.
17. A. Ashley Cooper. Cooper won the men's singles title at the Australian Open in 1957, marking his first victory in the tournament. He would only win it once more.

18. C. Althea Gibson. Gibson defeated Angela Mortimer in two sets, though neither woman would ever win the event again.

Did You Know?

Lew Hoad lost in the U.S. Open final in 1956, which cost him the Calendar Grand Slam.

CHAPTER 18:
THE 1960S

1. When did Rod Laver achieve his first Grand Slam by winning all four major titles in the same year?

    A. 1960
    B. 1962
    C. 1964
    D. 1966

2. Who won the men's singles title at Wimbledon in 1969, the first step in another Grand Slam?

    A. Rod Laver
    B. Ken Rosewall
    C. Roy Emerson
    D. John Newcombe

3. Which year marked the first Open Era Grand Slam tournament?

    A. 1966
    B. 1967
    C. 1968
    D. 1969

4. How many players participated in the men's singles tournament at the first Open Era Wimbledon Championships?

    A. 64
    B. 128
    C. 256
    D. 512

5. Who won the men's singles title at the U.S. National Championships in 1960, his second and final victory at the tournament?

    A. Rod Laver
    B. Neale Fraser
    C. Roy Emerson
    D. John Newcombe

6. Who was the first female tennis player to win the women's singles title at Wimbledon in the Open Era?

    A. Billie Jean King
    B. Margaret Court
    C. Maria Bueno
    D. Ann Jones

7. Tennis was included in the Olympics as a demonstration sport in which year?

    A. 1964
    B. 1968
    C. 1972
    D. 1976

8. Who won the men's singles title at the U.S. Pro Tennis Championships in 1963, his first time winning the tournament?

    A. Rod Laver
    B. Ken Rosewall
    C. Pancho González
    D. Tony Trabert

9. Who won the first men's singles title at the U.S. Open as part of the Open Era?

    A. Rod Laver
    B. Ken Rosewall
    C. Arthur Ashe
    D. John Newcombe

10. Which country won the Davis Cup in 1964, which was their eighth time winning?

    A. United States
    B. Great Britain
    C. Australia
    D. France

11. Who was the first player to win the men's singles titles at Wimbledon and the U.S. Open in the same year during the 1960s?

    A. Rod Laver
    B. Ken Rosewall
    C. Roy Emerson
    D. John Newcombe

12. Which player won the women's singles title at the Australian Open in 1965?

    A. Margaret Court
    B. Billie Jean King
    C. Maria Bueno
    D. Ann Jones

13. Which player won the men's singles title at Wimbledon in 1961, his first title at the event?

    A. Rod Laver
    B. Ken Rosewall
    C. Roy Emerson
    D. John Newcombe

14. Who was the first player to win the women's singles title at the U.S. Open in the Open Era?

    A. Billie Jean King
    B. Margaret Court
    C. Maria Bueno
    D. Ann Jones

15. How many times did Rod Laver win the men's singles title at Wimbledon in the 1960s?

    A. One
    B. Two
    C. Three
    D. Four

16. Who won the men's singles title at the U.S. Pro Tennis Championships in 1967, his second victory at the event?

    A. Rod Laver
    B. Ken Rosewall
    C. Pancho González
    D. Tony Trabert

17. Which player won the men's singles title at the Australian Open in 1965, marking his fourth victory at the event?

    A. Rod Laver
    B. Ken Rosewall
    C. Roy Emerson
    D. John Newcombe

18. Who won the women's singles title at Wimbledon in 1966, marking her first victory in the tournament?

    A. Billie Jean King
    B. Margaret Court
    C. Maria Bueno
    D. Ann Jones

Chapter 18 Answers:

1. B. 1962. Rod Laver achieved his first Grand Slam in 1962, winning all four major titles (Australian Open, French Open, Wimbledon, and U.S. Open) in a single calendar year. This remarkable feat established him as one of the greatest tennis players of all time.
2. A. Rod Laver. Laver won the men's singles title at Wimbledon in 1969, marking his second Grand Slam. He is the only player to have won two Grand Slams, solidifying his legacy in tennis history.
3. C. 1968. The first Open Era Grand Slam tournament was held in 1968, starting with the French Open. This era allowed both amateur and professional players to compete, revolutionizing the sport.
4. B. 128. One hundred twenty-eight players participated in the men's singles tournament at the first Open Era Wimbledon Championships in 1968.
5. B. Neale Fraser. Fraser defeated Rod Laver in straight sets in the final to win the tournament.
6. A. Billie Jean King. King was the first female tennis player to win the women's singles title at Wimbledon in the Open Era, achieving this in 1968. Her victory was a milestone for women's tennis.
7. B. 1968. Tennis was included in the Olympics as a demonstration sport in 1968, held in Mexico City. This inclusion highlighted the sport's growing global popularity.
8. B. Ken Rosewall. Rosewall won the men's singles title at the U.S. Pro Tennis Championships in 1963, marking his first victory in the tournament. His win was part of his impressive career in professional tennis.
9. C. Arthur Ashe. Ashe won the men's singles title at the U.S. Open in 1968, marking the first Open Era victory in the tournament. He was the first African American man to win a Grand Slam title.
10. C. Australia. Australia won the Davis Cup in 1964, marking their eighth victory in the competition. This win underscored Australia's dominance in tennis during the 1960s.
11. A. Rod Laver. Laver was the first player to win the men's singles title at Wimbledon and the U.S. Open in the same year during the 1960s, achieving this in 1969 as part of his second Grand Slam.
12. A. Margaret Court. Court won the women's singles title at the Australian Open in 1965, marking her dominance in the tournament. She went on to win a total of 11 Australian Open singles titles.

13. C. Roy Emerson. Emerson won the men's singles title at Wimbledon in 1961, marking his first victory in the tournament. He went on to win 12 Grand Slam singles titles in his career.
14. A. Billie Jean King. King was the first female tennis player to win the women's singles title at the U.S. Open in the Open Era, achieving this in 1968. Her victory was a significant milestone for women's tennis.
15. C. Three. Rod Laver won the men's singles title at Wimbledon three times in the 1960s, in 1961, 1962, and 1969. His consistent performance highlighted his dominance in the sport.
16. A. Rod Laver. Laver won the men's singles title at the U.S. Pro Tennis Championships in 1967, marking his second victory in the tournament. His win was part of his remarkable career in professional tennis.
17. C. Roy Emerson. Emerson won the men's singles title at the Australian Open in 1965, marking his fourth victory in the tournament. His achievement contributed to his legacy as one of the greatest players of his era.
18. A. Billie Jean King. King won the women's singles title at Wimbledon in 1966, marking her first victory in the tournament. Her win was a significant milestone in her illustrious career.

Did You Know?

Billie Jean King is considered one of the greatest tennis players in history. She even won 11 career Grand Slam mixed doubles tournaments.

CHAPTER 19:
THE 1970S

1. In which year did Margaret Court achieve her Grand Slam, winning all four major titles in a single calendar year?

    A. 1970
    B. 1972
    C. 1974
    D. 1976

2. Who won the men's singles title at Wimbledon in 1975, which was his first victory at the tournament?

    A. Björn Borg
    B. Jimmy Connors
    C. Arthur Ashe
    D. John Newcombe

3. The first U.S. Open held on clay courts took place in which year?

    A. 1970
    B. 1973
    C. 1975
    D. 1978

4. How many players participated in the men's singles tournament at the 1970 U.S. Open?

    A. 64
    B. 128
    C. 256
    D. 512

5. Which player won the men's singles title at the 1974 French Open?

    A. Björn Borg
    B. Guillermo Vilas
    C. Ilie Năstase
    D. Jan Kodes

6. Who was the first player to win three women's singles titles at Wimbledon in the 1970s?

    A. Billie Jean King
    B. Chris Evert
    C. Evonne Goolagong
    D. Martina Navratilova

7. Who won the men's singles title at the Australian Open in 1977, which was his first victory in the tournament?

    A. Vitas Gerulaitis
    B. Ken Rosewall
    C. John Newcombe
    D. Roscoe Tanner

8. Which of these players, teamed with Arthur Ashe, won the men's doubles title at the first Australian Open in 1977?

    A. Tony Roche
    B. Charlie Pasarell
    C. Erik van Dillen
    D. John Alexander

9. Who won the men's singles title at the U.S. Open in 1978, the first held on hard courts?

    A. Jimmy Connors
    B. Björn Borg
    C. John McEnroe
    D. Guillermo Vilas

10. Which country won the Davis Cup in 1973, marking their first victory in the competition?

    A. United States
    B. Australia
    C. South Africa
    D. Sweden

11. Who was the first player to win the men's singles title at Wimbledon and the French Open in the same year during the 1970s?

    A. Björn Borg
    B. Jimmy Connors
    C. Ilie Năstase
    D. Guillermo Vilas

12. Which player won the women's singles title at the French Open in 1974, marking her first time winning the tournament?

    A. Chris Evert
    B. Billie Jean King
    C. Evonne Goolagong
    D. Martina Navratilova

13. Which player won the men's singles title at Wimbledon in 1976, his first victory in the tournament?

    A. Jimmy Connors
    B. John McEnroe
    C. Arthur Ashe
    D. Björn Borg

14. Who was the only player to win the women's singles title at the U.S. Open four times during the 1970s?

    A. Billie Jean King
    B. Chris Evert
    C. Tracy Austin
    D. Margaret Court

15. How many times did Björn Borg win the U.S. Open men's singles title during the 1970s?

    A. Zero
    B. One
    C. Two
    D. Three

16. Which of these players won his first doubles title at the French Open in 1973?

    A. Marty Riessen
    B. Frew McMillan
    C. Bob Hewitt
    D. Tom Okker

17. Which player won the men's singles title at the Australian Open in 1976, marking his first victory in the tournament?

    A. John Newcombe
    B. Ken Rosewall
    C. Jimmy Connors
    D. Mark Edmondson

18. Who won the women's singles title at Wimbledon in 1978?

    A. Billie Jean King
    B. Chris Evert
    C. Evonne Goolagong
    D. Martina Navratilova

Chapter 19 Answers:

1. A. 1970. Margaret Court achieved her Grand Slam in 1970, winning all four major titles (Australian Open, French Open, Wimbledon, and U.S. Open) in a single calendar year. She became the first woman in the Open Era to accomplish this feat.
2. C. Arthur Ashe. Ashe won the men's singles title at Wimbledon in 1975, marking his first victory in the tournament. His win was historic, as he became the first African American man to win Wimbledon.
3. C. 1975. The first U.S. Open held on clay courts took place in 1975. This change was part of the tournament's evolution before it switched to hard courts in 1978.
4. B. 128. One hundred twenty-eight players participated in the men's singles tournament at the 1970 U.S. Open.
5. A. Björn Borg. Borg won the men's singles title at the French Open in 1974, marking his first victory in the tournament. He went on to win six French Open titles in his career.
6. A. Billie Jean King. King was the first female tennis player to win the women's singles title at Wimbledon three times in the 1970s, achieving this in 1972, 1973, and 1975.
7. D. Roscoe Tanner. Tanner won the men's singles title at the Australian Open in 1977, marking his first victory in the tournament. His powerful serve was a key factor in his success.
8. A. Tony Roche. Roche and Ashe defeated Charlie Pasarell and Erik van Dillen in straight sets to win the title.
9. A. Jimmy Connors. Connors won the men's singles title at the U.S. Open in 1978, marking the first victory on hard courts. His win was part of his successful career in tennis.
10. C. South Africa. South Africa won the Davis Cup in 1973, marking their first victory in the competition. This win was a significant achievement for the country.
11. A. Björn Borg. Borg was the first player to win the men's singles title at Wimbledon and the French Open in the same year during the 1970s, achieving this in 1978 and 1979.
12. A. Chris Evert. Evert won the women's singles title at the French Open in 1974, marking her first victory in the tournament. She went on to win seven French Open titles in her career.
13. D. Björn Borg. It was his first of five titles at the tournament.

14. B. Chris Evert. Evert was the first female tennis player to win the women's singles title at the U.S. Open four times in the 1970s, achieving this in 1975, 1976, 1977, and 1978.
15. A. Zero. Borg did not capture a U.S. Open singles title, but he finished as the runner-up twice during the 1970s.
16. D. Tom Okker. He partnered with John Newcombe and defeated Jimmy Connors and Ilie Năstase in the final.
17. D. Mark Edmondson. Edmondson won the men's singles title at the Australian Open in 1976, marking his first victory in the tournament. His win was notable as he was the last Australian to win the title.
18. D. Martina Navratilova. Navratilova won the women's singles title at Wimbledon in 1978, marking her first victory in the tournament. Her win was a significant milestone in her illustrious career.

Did You Know?

Jimmy Connors was one French Open away from completing a Calendar Grand Slam in 1974, but his 109 career titles are the most of all time.

CHAPTER 20:
THE 1980S

1. In which year did Steffi Graf achieve her Golden Slam, winning all four majors and the Olympic gold in the same year?

    A. 1984
    B. 1986
    C. 1988
    D. 1989

2. Who won the men's singles title at Wimbledon in 1985, his first victory in the tournament?

    A. Boris Becker
    B. Stefan Edberg
    C. Ivan Lendl
    D. John McEnroe

3. Who won the men's singles title at the Australian Open in 1981, his first victory at the major event?

    A. Johan Kriek
    B. Ivan Lendl
    C. John McEnroe
    D. Mats Wilander

4. How many players participated in the men's singles tournament at the 1980 French Open?

    A. 64
    B. 128
    C. 256
    D. 512

5. Which player won the men's singles title at the Australian Open in 1983, his first victory at the major tournament?

    A. Mats Wilander
    B. Ivan Lendl
    C. John McEnroe
    D. Stefan Edberg

6. Which of these players won the women's singles title at Wimbledon six times in the 1980s?

    A. Chris Evert
    B. Steffi Graf
    C. Martina Navratilova
    D. Hana Mandlikova

7. Who won the men's singles title at the Australian Open in 1987, his second victory in the tournament?

   A. Stefan Edberg
   B. Mats Wilander
   C. Ivan Lendl
   D. Pat Cash

8. Who won the men's doubles title at the French Open in 1985?

   A. Mark Edmondson and Kim Warwick
   B. Shlomo Glickstein and Hans Simonsson
   C. Henri Leconte and Yannick Noah
   D. Anders Jarryd and Robert Seguso

9. Who won the men's singles title at the U.S. Open in 1988, his only win at the major event?

   A. Mats Wilander
   B. Ivan Lendl
   C. John McEnroe
   D. Stefan Edberg

10. Which country won the Davis Cup in 1980, their first time winning the competition?

    A. Czechoslovakia
    B. Australia
    C. Sweden
    D. France

11. Who was the first player to win the men's singles title at Wimbledon and the U.S. Open in the same year during the 1980s?

    A. Boris Becker
    B. Stefan Edberg
    C. Ivan Lendl
    D. John McEnroe

12. Who won the women's singles title at the French Open in 1987, her first win at the major event?

    A. Chris Evert
    B. Steffi Graf
    C. Martina Navratilova
    D. Hana Mandlikova

13. Which player won the men's singles title at Wimbledon in 1981, his first of three career titles at the major event?

    A. Boris Becker
    B. Stefan Edberg
    C. Ivan Lendl
    D. John McEnroe

14. Which of these players won the women's singles title at the U.S. Open four times during the 1980s?

    A. Chris Evert
    B. Steffi Graf
    C. Martina Navratilova
    D. Hana Mandlikova

15. How many times did John McEnroe win the men's singles title at Wimbledon in the 1980s?

    A. Two
    B. Three
    C. Four
    D. Five

16. Who won the men's doubles title at the Australian Open in 1984, thanks to partnering with Mark Edmondson?

    A. Sherwood Stewart
    B. Joakim Nystrom
    C. Mats Wilander
    D. Paul McNamee

17. Which player won the men's singles title at the French Open in 1982?

    A. Mats Wilander
    B. Ivan Lendl
    C. John McEnroe
    D. Stefan Edberg

18. Who won the women's singles title at Wimbledon in 1988?

    A. Chris Evert
    B. Steffi Graf
    C. Martina Navratilova
    D. Hana Mandlikova

Chapter 20 Answers:

1. C. 1988. Steffi Graf achieved her Golden Slam in 1988, winning all four major titles (Australian Open, French Open, Wimbledon, and U.S. Open) and the Olympic gold medal in a single calendar year. This remarkable feat established her as one of the greatest tennis players of all time.
2. A. Boris Becker. Becker won the men's singles title at Wimbledon in 1985, marking his first victory in the tournament. At 17, he became the youngest Wimbledon champion in history.
3. A. Johan Kriek. Kriek won the men's singles title at the Australian Open in 1981, and he would win it again one year later, in 1982.
4. B. 128. One hundred twenty-eight players participated in the men's singles tournament at the 1980 French Open.
5. A. Mats Wilander. Wilander won the men's singles title at the Australian Open in 1983, his first of three victories at the event.
6. C. Martina Navratilova. Navratilova was the only female tennis player to win the women's singles title at Wimbledon six times, achieving this remarkable feat from 1982 to 1987.
7. A. Stefan Edberg. Edberg won the men's singles title at the Australian Open in 1987, marking his second victory in the tournament. His first victory came in 1985.
8. D. Anders Jarryd and Robert Seguso. Jarryd and Seguso won the men's doubles title at the French Open in 1985, marking their first Grand Slam doubles victory.
9. A. Mats Wilander. Wilander won the men's singles title at the U.S. Open in 1988, marking his first victory in the tournament. His win was part of his impressive career in tennis.
10. C. Sweden. Sweden won the Davis Cup in 1981, marking their first victory in the competition. This win highlighted Sweden's emergence as a tennis powerhouse.
11. D. John McEnroe. McEnroe was the first player to win the men's singles title at Wimbledon and the U.S. Open in the same year during the 1980s, achieving this in 1981.
12. B. Steffi Graf. Graf won the women's singles title at the French Open in 1987, marking her first victory in the tournament. She went on to win 22 Grand Slam singles titles in her career.
13. D. John McEnroe. McEnroe won the men's singles title at Wimbledon in 1981, marking his first of three career victories at the event.

14. C. Martina Navratilova. Navratilova won the tournament four times in the 1980s, and she nearly made it five in a row but lost the 1985 final.
15. B. Three times. John McEnroe won the men's singles title at Wimbledon three times in the 1980s, in 1981, 1983, and 1984.
16. A. Sherwood Stewart. He joined Edmondson, who had won the event several times, to win the title in 1984.
17. A. Mats Wilander. Wilander won the men's singles title at the French Open in 1982, marking his first victory in the tournament. His win was part of his successful career in tennis.
18. B. Steffi Graf. Graf won the women's singles title at Wimbledon in 1988, marking her first victory in the tournament. She defeated Martina Navratilova in the final, who had won the tournament the previous six years.

Did You Know?

Steffi Graf, who dominated much of the 1980s and 1990s, was inducted into the International Tennis Hall of Fame in 2004.

CHAPTER 21:
THE 1990S

1. Who won the men's singles title at Wimbledon in 1992?

   A. Andre Agassi
   B. Pete Sampras
   C. Boris Becker
   D. Stefan Edberg

2. In which year did Steffi Graf win her last Grand Slam title?

   A. 1996
   B. 1997
   C. 1998
   D. 1999

3. Who won the men's singles title at the Australian Open in 1990?

   A. Ivan Lendl
   B. Stefan Edberg
   C. Jim Courier
   D. Pete Sampras

4. How many Grand Slam titles did Monica Seles win in the 1990s?

   A. Six
   B. Seven
   C. Eight
   D. Nine

5. Which player won the men's singles title at the French Open in 1997?

   A. Gustavo Kuerten
   B. Sergi Bruguera
   C. Yevgeny Kafelnikov
   D. Thomas Muster

6. Who won the women's singles title at Wimbledon in 1994?

   A. Steffi Graf
   B. Martina Navratilova
   C. Conchita Martínez
   D. Jana Novotná

7. Who won the men's singles title at the U.S. Open in 1990?

   A. Pete Sampras
   B. Andre Agassi
   C. Boris Becker
   D. Stefan Edberg

8. Who won the women's singles title at the Australian Open in 1990?

    A. Steffi Graf
    B. Monica Seles
    C. Arantxa Sánchez-Vicario
    D. Mary Pierce

9. Which country won the Davis Cup in 1995?

    A. United States
    B. Sweden
    C. Germany
    D. Russia

10. Who won the men's singles title at Wimbledon in 1996?

    A. Richard Krajicek
    B. Pete Sampras
    C. Andre Agassi
    D. Goran Ivanišević

11. Who won the women's singles title at the French Open in 1990?

    A. Steffi Graf
    B. Monica Seles
    C. Arantxa Sánchez-Vicario
    D. Gabriela Sabatini

12. Who won the men's singles title at the Australian Open in 1995?

    A. Andre Agassi
    B. Pete Sampras
    C. Boris Becker
    D. Jim Courier

13. Who won the women's singles title at the French Open in 1996?

    A. Martina Hingis
    B. Venus Williams
    C. Lindsay Davenport
    D. Arantxa Sánchez-Vicario

14. How many times did Pete Sampras win the Wimbledon men's singles title during the 1990s?

    A. Four
    B. Five
    C. Six
    D. Seven

15. Who won the men's singles title at the French Open in 1996?

    A. Yevgeny Kafelnikov
    B. Thomas Muster
    C. Gustavo Kuerten
    D. Sergi Bruguera

16. Who won the women's singles title at Wimbledon in 1998, her first victory at that Grand Slam event?

    A. Jana Novotná
    B. Steffi Graf
    C. Martina Hingis
    D. Lindsay Davenport

17. Who won the men's singles title at the U.S. Open in 1994, his first Grand Slam victory at that event?

    A. Andre Agassi
    B. Pete Sampras
    C. Patrick Rafter
    D. Michael Stich

18. Which player won the women's singles title at the Australian Open in 1999?

    A. Martina Hingis
    B. Lindsay Davenport
    C. Serena Williams
    D. Venus Williams

Chapter 21 Answers:

1. A. Andre Agassi. Agassi won the men's singles title at Wimbledon in 1992, marking his first victory at the tournament. His win was a significant milestone in his career.
2. D. 1999. Steffi Graf won her last Grand Slam title at the French Open in 1999, capping off an illustrious career with 22 Grand Slam singles titles.
3. B. Stefan Edberg. Edberg won the men's singles title at the Australian Open in 1990, marking his first victory at the tournament in the 1990s.
4. C. Eight. Monica Seles won eight Grand Slam singles titles in the 1990s, showcasing her dominance in women's tennis during the decade.
5. A. Gustavo Kuerten. Kuerten won the men's singles title at the French Open in 1997, marking his first Grand Slam victory and the beginning of his success on clay courts.
6. C. Conchita Martínez. Martínez won the women's singles title at Wimbledon in 1994, marking her first victory at the tournament.
7. A. Pete Sampras. Sampras won the men's singles title at the U.S. Open in 1990, marking his first Grand Slam victory and the start of his legendary career.
8. B. Monica Seles. Seles won the women's singles title at the Australian Open in 1991, marking her first victory at the tournament in the 1990s.
9. A. United States. They defeated Russia in the final of the tournament.
10. A. Richard Krajicek. Krajicek won the men's singles title at Wimbledon in 1996, marking his first victory at the tournament.
11. D. Gabriela Sabatini. Sabatini won the women's singles title at the French Open in 1990, marking her first Grand Slam victory.
12. A. Andre Agassi. Agassi won the men's singles title at the Australian Open in 1995, marking his first victory at the tournament.
13. A. Martina Hingis. Hingis won the women's singles title at the U.S. Open in 1997, marking her first Grand Slam victory.
14. C. Six. Pete Sampras won the Wimbledon men's singles title six times in the 1990s, highlighting his dominance at the tournament. He won it one more time in 2000.
15. A. Yevgeny Kafelnikov. Kafelnikov won the men's singles title at the French Open in 1996, marking his first Grand Slam victory.
16. A. Jana Novotná. Novotná won the women's singles title at Wimbledon in 1998, marking her first victory at the tournament.

17. A. Andre Agassi. Agassi won the men's singles title at the U.S. Open in 1994, though his first Grand Slam came two years earlier at Wimbledon.
18. B. Lindsay Davenport. Davenport won the women's singles title at the Australian Open in 1999, marking her first Grand Slam victory.

Did You Know?

Boris Becker is the youngest-ever Wimbledon singles champion, winning at 17 years old.

CHAPTER 22:
THE 2000S

1. Who won the men's singles title at Wimbledon in 2001?

    A. Pete Sampras
    B. Roger Federer
    C. Goran Ivanišević
    D. Lleyton Hewitt

2. In which year did Serena Williams complete her first "Serena Slam" by holding all four Grand Slam titles at the same time?

    A. 2001
    B. 2002
    C. 2003
    D. 2004

3. Who won the men's singles title at the Australian Open in 2004?

    A. Andre Agassi
    B. Roger Federer
    C. Marat Safin
    D. Andy Roddick

4. How many Grand Slam titles did Rafael Nadal win in the 2000s?

    A. Four
    B. Six
    C. Eight
    D. Ten

5. Which player won the women's singles title at the French Open in 2005?

    A. Justine Henin
    B. Serena Williams
    C. Maria Sharapova
    D. Amélie Mauresmo

6. Who won the men's singles title at Wimbledon in 2008?

    A. Roger Federer
    B. Rafael Nadal
    C. Novak Djokovic
    D. Andy Murray

7. Which player won the women's singles title at the U.S. Open in 2000?

    A. Venus Williams
    B. Serena Williams

C. Lindsay Davenport
   D. Martina Hingis

8. Who won the men's singles title at the 2000 Australian Open?

   A. Andre Agassi
   B. Pete Sampras
   C. Marat Safin
   D. Roger Federer

9. Which country won the Davis Cup in 2004?

   A. United States
   B. Spain
   C. Russia
   D. Australia

10. Who won the men's singles title at Wimbledon in 2003?

    A. Pete Sampras
    B. Roger Federer
    C. Andy Roddick
    D. Lleyton Hewitt

11. Which player won the women's singles title at the French Open in 2001?

    A. Jennifer Capriati
    B. Serena Williams
    C. Justine Henin
    D. Kim Clijsters

12. Who won the men's singles title at the Australian Open in 2009?

    A. Rafael Nadal
    B. Roger Federer
    C. Novak Djokovic
    D. Andy Murray

13. Which player won the women's singles title at the U.S. Open in 2006?

    A. Maria Sharapova
    B. Serena Williams
    C. Justine Henin
    D. Kim Clijsters

14. How many times did Roger Federer win the Wimbledon men's singles title in the 2000s?

A. Four
B. Five
C. Six
D. Seven

15. Who won the men's singles title at the French Open in 2004?

    A. Gastón Gaudio
    B. Rafael Nadal
    C. Roger Federer
    D. Juan Carlos Ferrero

16. Which player won the women's singles title at Wimbledon in 2007?

    A. Venus Williams
    B. Serena Williams
    C. Maria Sharapova
    D. Amélie Mauresmo

17. Who won the men's singles title in the U.S. Open in 2003?

    A. Andy Roddick
    B. Roger Federer
    C. Lleyton Hewitt
    D. Marat Safin

18. Which player won the women's singles title at the Australian Open in 2008?

    A. Maria Sharapova
    B. Serena Williams
    C. Justine Henin
    D. Ana Ivanović

Chapter 22 Answers:

1. C. Goran Ivanišević. Ivanišević won the men's singles title at Wimbledon in 2001. He was known for his powerful serve but only won one Grand Slam singles title in his career.
2. B. 2002. Serena Williams achieved her first "Serena Slam" by holding all four Grand Slam titles simultaneously in 2002. Serena won a total of 23 Grand Slam singles titles in her career.
3. B. Roger Federer. Federer won the men's singles title at the Australian Open in 2004. He won a total of 20 Grand Slam singles titles in his career.
4. B. Six. Rafael Nadal won six Grand Slam singles titles in the 2000s. He won a total of 22 Grand Slam singles titles in his career.
5. A. Justine Henin. Henin won the women's singles title at the French Open in 2005. She won a total of seven Grand Slam singles titles in her career.
6. B. Rafael Nadal. Nadal won the men's singles title at Wimbledon in 2008.
7. A. Venus Williams. Williams won the women's singles title at the U.S. Open in 2000. She won a total of seven Grand Slam singles titles in her career.
8. A. Andre Agassi. Agassi won the men's singles title at the Australian Open in 2000. He won a total of eight Grand Slam singles titles in his career.
9. B. Spain. Spain won the Davis Cup in 2004. This victory marked their second Davis Cup title.
10. B. Roger Federer. Federer won the men's singles title at Wimbledon in 2003.
11. A. Jennifer Capriati. Capriati won the women's singles title at the French Open in 2001. She won a total of three Grand Slam singles titles in her career.
12. A. Rafael Nadal. Nadal won the men's singles title at the Australian Open in 2009.
13. A. Maria Sharapova. Sharapova won the women's singles title at the U.S. Open in 2006. She won a total of five Grand Slam singles titles in her career.
14. B. Five times. Roger Federer won the Wimbledon men's singles title five times in the 2000s. He won a total of 20 Grand Slam singles titles in his career.

15. A. Gastón Gaudio. Gaudio won the men's singles title at the French Open in 2004. This was his only Grand Slam singles title.
16. A. Venus Williams. Williams won the women's singles title at Wimbledon in 2007.
17. A. Andy Roddick. Roddick won the men's singles title at the U.S. Open in 2003. It was the only Grand Slam win in his career.
18. A. Maria Sharapova. Sharapova won the women's singles title at the Australian Open in 2008.

Did You Know?

Marat Safin only won two Grand Slam titles in his career, but he was ranked No. 1 in November 2000.

CHAPTER 23:
THE 2010S

1. Who won the men's singles title at Wimbledon in 2013?

   A. Novak Djokovic
   B. Andy Murray
   C. Roger Federer
   D. Rafael Nadal

2. In which year did Serena Williams achieve her second "Serena Slam"?

   A. 2012
   B. 2013
   C. 2014
   D. 2015

3. Who won the men's singles title at the Australian Open in 2012?

   A. Novak Djokovic
   B. Roger Federer
   C. Rafael Nadal
   D. Andy Murray

4. How many Grand Slam titles did Novak Djokovic win in the 2010s?

   A. Ten
   B. 12
   C. 14
   D. 16

5. Which player won the women's singles title at the French Open in 2016?

   A. Serena Williams
   B. Garbiñe Muguruza
   C. Simona Halep
   D. Maria Sharapova

6. Who won the men's singles title at Wimbledon in 2017?

   A. Roger Federer
   B. Novak Djokovic
   C. Andy Murray
   D. Rafael Nadal

7. Which player won the women's singles title at the U.S. Open in 2018?

   A. Naomi Osaka
   B. Serena Williams

C. Sloane Stephens
D. Simona Halep

8. Who won the men's singles gold medal at the 2012 London Olympics?

    A. Andy Murray
    B. Roger Federer
    C. Novak Djokovic
    D. Rafael Nadal

9. Which country won the Davis Cup in 2010?

    A. Spain
    B. Serbia
    C. France
    D. Czech Republic

10. Who won the men's singles title at Wimbledon in 2010?

    A. Rafael Nadal
    B. Roger Federer
    C. Novak Djokovic
    D. Andy Murray

11. Which player won the women's singles title at the French Open in 2014?

    A. Maria Sharapova
    B. Serena Williams
    C. Simona Halep
    D. Garbiñe Muguruza

12. Who won the men's singles title at the Australian Open in 2019?

    A. Novak Djokovic
    B. Roger Federer
    C. Rafael Nadal
    D. Andy Murray

13. Which player won the women's singles title at the U.S. Open in 2017?

    A. Sloane Stephens
    B. Serena Williams
    C. Madison Keys
    D. Simona Halep

14. How many times did Rafael Nadal win the French Open men's singles title during the 2010s?

    A. Five
    B. Six
    C. Seven
    D. Eight

15. Who won the men's singles title at the French Open in 2015?

    A. Novak Djokovic
    B. Rafael Nadal
    C. Stan Wawrinka
    D. Roger Federer

16. Which player won the women's singles title at Wimbledon in 2011?

    A. Petra Kvitová
    B. Serena Williams
    C. Maria Sharapova
    D. Simona Halep

17. Who won the men's singles title at the U.S. Open in 2016?

    A. Stan Wawrinka
    B. Novak Djokovic
    C. Andy Murray
    D. Rafael Nadal

18. Which country won the Fed Cup in 2018?

    A. United States
    B. Czech Republic
    C. France
    D. Russia

Chapter 23 Answers:

1. B. Andy Murray. Murray won the men's singles title at Wimbledon in 2013, becoming the first British man to win the title since 1936. He won a total of three Grand Slam singles titles in his career.
2. D. 2015. Serena Williams achieved her second "Serena Slam" by holding all four Grand Slam titles simultaneously in 2015.
3. A. Novak Djokovic. Djokovic won the men's singles title at the Australian Open in 2012. He won a total of 20 Grand Slam singles titles in his career.
4. B. 12. Novak Djokovic won 12 Grand Slam singles titles in the 2010s.
5. B. Garbiñe Muguruza. Muguruza won the women's singles title at the French Open in 2016. She won a total of two Grand Slam singles titles in her career.
6. A. Roger Federer. Federer won the men's singles title at Wimbledon in 2017.
7. A. Naomi Osaka. Osaka won the women's singles title at the U.S. Open in 2018. She won a total of four Grand Slam singles titles in her career.
8. A. Andy Murray. Murray won the men's singles gold medal at the 2012 London Olympics. He won a total of three Grand Slam singles titles in his career.
9. B. Serbia. Serbia won the Davis Cup in 2010, marking their first victory in the competition.
10. A. Rafael Nadal. Nadal won the men's singles title at Wimbledon in 2010.
11. A. Maria Sharapova. Sharapova won the women's singles title at the French Open in 2014.
12. A. Novak Djokovic. Djokovic won the men's singles title at the Australian Open in 2019. He won a total of 20 Grand Slam singles titles in his career.
13. A. Sloane Stephens. Stephens won the women's singles title at the U.S. Open in 2017. She won one Grand Slam singles title in her career.
14. B. Six times. Rafael Nadal won the French Open men's singles title six times in the 2010s.
15. C. Stan Wawrinka. Wawrinka won the men's singles title at the French Open in 2015. He won a total of three Grand Slam singles titles in his career.

16. A. Petra Kvitová. Kvitová won the women's singles title at Wimbledon in 2011. She won a total of two Grand Slam singles titles in her career.
17. A. Stan Wawrinka. Wawrinka won the men's singles title at the U.S. Open in 2016.
18. B. Czech Republic. Czech Republic won the Fed Cup in 2018, marking their sixth victory in the competition during the decade.

Did You Know?

Serena Williams first reached the top ranking in July 2002, and her 73 career wins is fifth all-time.

CHAPTER 24:
2020–2024

1. Who won the men's singles title at the U.S. Open in 2020?
   A. Dominic Thiem
   B. Novak Djokovic
   C. Daniil Medvedev
   D. Alexander Zverev

2. In which year did Ashleigh Barty win her first Wimbledon singles title?
   A. 2020
   B. 2021
   C. 2022
   D. 2023

3. Who won the men's singles title at the Australian Open in 2021?
   A. Novak Djokovic
   B. Rafael Nadal
   C. Daniil Medvedev
   D. Stefanos Tsitsipas

4. How many Grand Slam singles titles did Iga Świątek win between 2020 and 2024?
   A. Two
   B. Three
   C. Four
   D. Five

5. Which player won the women's singles title at the French Open in 2022?
   A. Iga Świątek
   B. Barbora Krejčíková
   C. Simona Halep
   D. Naomi Osaka

6. Who won the men's singles title at Wimbledon in 2022?
   A. Novak Djokovic
   B. Rafael Nadal
   C. Carlos Alcaraz
   D. Matteo Berrettini

7. Which player won the women's singles title at the U.S. Open in 2021?
   A. Emma Raducanu
   B. Leylah Fernandez

C. Naomi Osaka
   D. Serena Williams

8. Who won the men's singles gold medal at the 2024 Paris Olympics?

   A. Novak Djokovic
   B. Alexander Zverev
   C. Daniil Medvedev
   D. Stefanos Tsitsipas

9. Which country won the Davis Cup in 2021?

   A. Spain
   B. Russia
   C. France
   D. Canada

10. Who won the men's singles title at Wimbledon in 2023?

    A. Novak Djokovic
    B. Carlos Alcaraz
    C. Daniil Medvedev
    D. Jannik Sinner

11. Which player won the women's singles title at the French Open in 2020?

    A. Iga Świątek
    B. Sofia Kenin
    C. Simona Halep
    D. Garbiñe Muguruza

12. Who won the men's singles title at the Australian Open in 2024?

    A. Novak Djokovic
    B. Daniil Medvedev
    C. Carlos Alcaraz
    D. Jannik Sinner

13. Which player won the women's singles title at the U.S. Open in 2022?

    A. Iga Świątek
    B. Emma Raducanu
    C. Leylah Fernandez
    D. Naomi Osaka

14. How many times did Novak Djokovic win the Australian Open men's singles title from 2020 to 2024?

- A. Two
- B. Three
- C. Four
- D. Five

15. Who won the men's singles title at the French Open in 2021?

    - A. Rafael Nadal
    - B. Novak Djokovic
    - C. Dominic Thiem
    - D. Stefanos Tsitsipas

16. Which player won the women's singles title at Wimbledon in 2023?

    - A. Ashleigh Barty
    - B. Iga Świątek
    - C. Simona Halep
    - D. Marketa Vondrousova

17. Who won the men's singles title at the U.S. Open in 2023?

    - A. Carlos Alcaraz
    - B. Daniil Medvedev
    - C. Novak Djokovic
    - D. Jannik Sinner

18. Which country won the Billie Jean King Cup in 2022?

    - A. United States
    - B. Russia
    - C. Czech Republic
    - D. Switzerland

Chapter 24 Answers:

1. A. Dominic Thiem. Thiem won the men's singles title at the U.S. Open in 2020. He won one Grand Slam singles title in his career.
2. B. 2021. Ashleigh Barty won her first Wimbledon singles title in 2021. She won a total of three Grand Slam singles titles in her career.
3. A. Novak Djokovic. Djokovic won the men's singles title at the Australian Open in 2021.
4. C. Four. Iga Świątek won four Grand Slam singles titles between 2020 and 2024.
5. A. Iga Świątek. Świątek won the women's singles title at the French Open in 2022.
6. A. Novak Djokovic. Djokovic won the men's singles title at Wimbledon in 2022.
7. A. Emma Raducanu. Raducanu won the women's singles title at the U.S. Open in 2021. She won one Grand Slam singles title in her career.
8. B. Alexander Zverev. Zverev won the men's singles gold medal at the 2021 Tokyo Olympics, though he had not yet won a Grand Slam title.
9. B. Russia. Russia won the Davis Cup in 2021, marking their third victory in the competition.
10. B. Carlos Alcaraz. Alcaraz won the men's singles title at Wimbledon in 2023. He has won a total of two Grand Slam singles titles in his career.
11. A. Iga Świątek. Świątek won the women's singles title at the French Open in 2020.
12. D. Jannik Sinner. Sinner won the men's singles title at the Australian Open in 2024.
13. A. Iga Świątek. Świątek won the women's singles title at the U.S. Open in 2022.
14. B. Three. Novak Djokovic won the Australian Open men's singles title three times between 2020 and 2024.
15. B. Novak Djokovic. Djokovic won the men's singles title at the French Open in 2021.
16. D. Marketa Vondrousova. Vondrousova won the women's singles title at Wimbledon in 2023.
17. A. Carlos Alcaraz. Alcaraz won the men's singles title at the U.S. Open in 2023.
18. D. Switzerland. Switzerland won the Billie Jean King Cup in 2022, marking their first victory in the competition.

Did You Know?

Novak Djokovic has won 72 big titles in his career, which is most of any player in tennis history.

CHAPTER 25:
MODERN WIMBLEDON

1. Who won the men's singles title at Wimbledon in 2008, ending Roger Federer's five-year winning streak at the tournament?

    A. Rafael Nadal
    B. Novak Djokovic
    C. Andy Murray
    D. Roger Federer

2. In which year did Serena Williams win her seventh Wimbledon singles title?

    A. 2012
    B. 2014
    C. 2016
    D. 2018

3. Who won the men's singles title at Wimbledon in 2013, becoming the first British man to win the title since 1936?

    A. Andy Murray
    B. Roger Federer
    C. Novak Djokovic
    D. Rafael Nadal

4. How many Wimbledon singles titles did Venus Williams win between 2004 and 2024?

    A. Two
    B. Three
    C. Four
    D. Five

5. Which player won the women's singles title at Wimbledon in 2011?

    A. Petra Kvitová
    B. Serena Williams
    C. Maria Sharapova
    D. Simona Halep

6. Who won the men's singles title at Wimbledon in 2019?

    A. Novak Djokovic
    B. Roger Federer
    C. Rafael Nadal
    D. Andy Murray

7. Which player won the women's singles title at Wimbledon in 2018, collecting her seventh title at the tournament?

   A. Angelique Kerber
   B. Serena Williams
   C. Simona Halep
   D. Garbiñe Muguruza

8. Who won the men's singles title at Wimbledon in 2022?

   A. Novak Djokovic
   B. Roger Federer
   C. Rafael Nadal
   D. Andy Murray

9. Which player won the women's singles title at Wimbledon in 2019, defeating Serena Williams in the final?

   A. Simona Halep
   B. Angelique Kerber
   C. Garbiñe Muguruza
   D. Petra Kvitová

10. Who won the men's singles title at Wimbledon in 2004?

    A. Roger Federer
    B. Rafael Nadal
    C. Andy Roddick
    D. Novak Djokovic

11. Which player won the women's singles title at Wimbledon in 2021?

    A. Ashleigh Barty
    B. Simona Halep
    C. Naomi Osaka
    D. Garbiñe Muguruza

12. How many times did Novak Djokovic win the Wimbledon men's singles title between 2004 and 2024?

    A. Five
    B. Six
    C. Seven
    D. Eight

13. Who won the men's singles title at Wimbledon in 2016?

    A. Andy Murray
    B. Novak Djokovic

    C. Roger Federer
    D. Rafael Nadal

14. Which player won the women's singles title at Wimbledon in 2014?

    A. Petra Kvitová
    B. Serena Williams
    C. Maria Sharapova
    D. Simona Halep

15. Who won the men's singles title at Wimbledon in 2023, defeating Novak Djokovic in the final?

    A. Carlos Alcaraz
    B. Daniil Medvedev
    C. Rafael Nadal
    D. Jannik Sinner

16. Which player won the women's singles title at Wimbledon in 2023?

    A. Marketa Vondrousova
    B. Iga Świątek
    C. Simona Halep
    D. Ashleigh Barty

17. Who won the men's singles title at Wimbledon in 2010?

    A. Rafael Nadal
    B. Roger Federer
    C. Novak Djokovic
    D. Andy Murray

18. Which player won the women's singles title at Wimbledon in 2006?

    A. Amélie Mauresmo
    B. Serena Williams
    C. Maria Sharapova
    D. Venus Williams

Chapter 25 Answers:

1. A. Rafael Nadal. Nadal won the men's singles title at Wimbledon in 2008, ending Roger Federer's five-year winning streak.
2. C. 2016. Serena Williams won her seventh Wimbledon singles title in 2016.
3. A. Andy Murray. Murray won the men's singles title at Wimbledon in 2013, becoming the first British man to win the title since 1936.
4. B. Three. Venus Williams won three Wimbledon singles titles between 2004 and 2024.
5. A. Petra Kvitová. Kvitová won the women's singles title at Wimbledon in 2011, marking her first Grand Slam victory.
6. A. Novak Djokovic. Djokovic won the men's singles title at Wimbledon in 2019, in a historic final that lasted nearly five hours.
7. A. Angelique Kerber. Kerber won the women's singles title at Wimbledon in 2018, her third Grand Slam victory. She won a total of three Grand Slam singles titles in her career.
8. A. Novak Djokovic. Djokovic won the men's singles title at Wimbledon in 2022, marking his seventh victory at the tournament.
9. A. Simona Halep. Halep won the women's singles title at Wimbledon in 2019, defeating Serena Williams in the final. She retired in 2025 and won a total of two Grand Slam singles titles in her career.
10. A. Roger Federer. Federer won the men's singles title at Wimbledon in 2004, starting a period of dominance at the tournament. He retired in 2022.
11. A. Ashleigh Barty. Barty won the women's singles title at Wimbledon in 2021, marking her second Grand Slam victory. She retired in 2022 and won a total of three Grand Slam singles titles in her career.
12. C. Seven times. Novak Djokovic won the Wimbledon men's singles title seven times between 2004 and 2024.
13. A. Andy Murray. Murray won the men's singles title at Wimbledon in 2016, marking his second victory at the tournament. He retired in 2024 and won a total of three Grand Slam singles titles in his career.
14. A. Petra Kvitová. Kvitová won the women's singles title at Wimbledon in 2014, marking her second Grand Slam victory.
15. A. Carlos Alcaraz. Alcaraz won the men's singles title at Wimbledon in 2023, defeating Novak Djokovic in the final.
16. A. Marketa Vondrousova. Vondrousova won the women's singles title at Wimbledon in 2023.

17. A. Rafael Nadal. Nadal won the men's singles title at Wimbledon in 2010.
18. A. Amélie Mauresmo. Mauresmo won the women's singles title at Wimbledon in 2006. She won a total of two Grand Slam singles titles in her career.

Did You Know?

The 2024 Wimbledon Championships awarded 50 million British pounds in prize money.

CHAPTER 26:
MODERN U.S. OPEN

1. Who won the men's singles title at the U.S. Open in 2009, ending Roger Federer's five-year winning streak?

    A. Rafael Nadal
    B. Novak Djokovic
    C. Andy Murray
    D. Juan Martín del Potro

2. In which year did Serena Williams win her sixth U.S. Open singles title?

    A. 2012
    B. 2013
    C. 2014
    D. 2015

3. Who won the men's singles title at the U.S. Open in 2012?

    A. Andy Murray
    B. Novak Djokovic
    C. Rafael Nadal
    D. Roger Federer

4. How many U.S. Open singles titles did Venus Williams win between 2004 and 2024?

    A. Zero
    B. One
    C. Two
    D. Three

5. Which player won the women's singles title at the U.S. Open in 2017?

    A. Sloane Stephens
    B. Serena Williams
    C. Naomi Osaka
    D. Simona Halep

6. Who won the men's singles title at the U.S. Open in 2019, including a thrilling five-set final?

    A. Novak Djokovic
    B. Roger Federer
    C. Rafael Nadal
    D. Dominic Thiem

7. Which player won the women's singles title at the U.S. Open in 2018?

     A. Naomi Osaka
     B. Serena Williams
     C. Simona Halep
     D. Angelique Kerber

8. Who won the men's singles title at the U.S. Open in 2020?

     A. Dominic Thiem
     B. Alexander Zverev
     C. Daniil Medvedev
     D. Stefanos Tsitsipas

9. Which player won the women's singles title at the U.S. Open in 2021?

     A. Emma Raducanu
     B. Leylah Fernandez
     C. Naomi Osaka
     D. Serena Williams

10. Who won the men's singles title at the U.S. Open in 2022?

     A. Carlos Alcaraz
     B. Novak Djokovic
     C. Rafael Nadal
     D. Daniil Medvedev

11. Which player won the women's singles title at the U.S. Open in 2022?

     A. Iga Świątek
     B. Emma Raducanu
     C. Leylah Fernandez
     D. Naomi Osaka

12. Who won the men's singles title at the U.S. Open in 2023?

     A. Carlos Alcaraz
     B. Novak Djokovic
     C. Rafael Nadal
     D. Jannik Sinner

13. Which player won the women's singles title at the U.S. Open in 2023?

     A. Aryna Sabalenka
     B. Emma Raducanu
     C. Leylah Fernandez
     D. Jessica Pegula

14. How many times did Novak Djokovic win the U.S. Open men's singles title between 2004 and 2024?

    A. Two
    B. Three
    C. Four
    D. Five

15. Who won the men's singles title at the U.S. Open in 2016?

    A. Stan Wawrinka
    B. Rafael Nadal
    C. Andy Murray
    D. Roger Federer

16. Which player won the women's singles title at the U.S. Open in 2014?

    A. Serena Williams
    B. Maria Sharapova
    C. Simona Halep
    D. Petra Kvitová

17. Who won the men's singles title at the U.S. Open in 2010?

    A. Rafael Nadal
    B. Roger Federer
    C. Novak Djokovic
    D. Andy Murray

18. Which player won the women's singles title at the U.S. Open in 2006?

    A. Maria Sharapova
    B. Serena Williams
    C. Justine Henin
    D. Amélie Mauresmo

Chapter 26 Answers:

1. D. Juan Martín del Potro. Del Potro won the men's singles title at the U.S. Open in 2009, ending Roger Federer's five-year winning streak. He won one Grand Slam singles title in his career.
2. C. 2014. Serena Williams won her sixth U.S. Open singles title in 2014.
3. A. Andy Murray. Murray won the men's singles title at the U.S. Open in 2012, marking his first Grand Slam victory.
4. A. Zero. Venus Williams did not win any U.S. Open singles titles between 2004 and 2024.
5. A. Sloane Stephens. Stephens won the women's singles title at the U.S. Open in 2017, marking her first Grand Slam victory.
6. C. Rafael Nadal. Nadal won the men's singles title at the U.S. Open in 2019, in a five-set thriller against Daniil Medvedev.
7. A. Naomi Osaka. Osaka won the women's singles title at the U.S. Open in 2018, her first Grand Slam victory.
8. A. Dominic Thiem. Thiem won the men's singles title at the U.S. Open in 2020, marking his first Grand Slam victory.
9. A. Emma Raducanu. Raducanu won the women's singles title at the U.S. Open in 2021, making history as the first qualifier to win a Grand Slam.
10. A. Carlos Alcaraz. Alcaraz won the men's singles title at the U.S. Open in 2022, defeating Casper Ruud in the final.
11. A. Iga Świątek. Świątek won the women's singles title at the U.S. Open in 2022, marking her third Grand Slam victory.
12. A. Carlos Alcaraz. Alcaraz won the men's singles title at the U.S. Open in 2023, defeating Daniil Medvedev in the final.
13. A. Aryna Sabalenka. Sabalenka won the women's singles title at the U.S. Open in 2023, marking her second Grand Slam victory.
14. B. Three. Novak Djokovic won the U.S. Open men's singles title three times between 2004 and 2024.
15. A. Stan Wawrinka. Wawrinka won the men's singles title at the U.S. Open in 2016, defeating Novak Djokovic in the final.
16. A. Serena Williams. Williams won the women's singles title at the U.S. Open in 2014, marking her 18th Grand Slam singles victory.
17. A. Rafael Nadal. Nadal won the men's singles title at the U.S. Open in 2010, completing his career Grand Slam.
18. A. Maria Sharapova. Sharapova won the women's singles title at the U.S. Open in 2006, marking her second Grand Slam victory.

Did You Know?

The 2024 U.S. Open awarded $75 million as prize money for the tournament.

CHAPTER 27: MODERN FRENCH OPEN

1. Who won the men's singles title at the French Open in 2005?

    A. Roger Federer
    B. Rafael Nadal
    C. Novak Djokovic
    D. Andy Murray

2. In which year did Serena Williams win her third French Open singles title?

    A. 2013
    B. 2014
    C. 2015
    D. 2016

3. Who captured the men's singles title at the French Open in 2016?

    A. Stan Wawrinka
    B. Rafael Nadal
    C. Andy Murray
    D. Roger Federer

4. How many French Open singles titles did Maria Sharapova win between 2004 and 2024?

    A. One
    B. Two
    C. Three
    D. Four

5. Which player won the women's singles title at the French Open in 2018?

    A. Simona Halep
    B. Serena Williams
    C. Garbiñe Muguruza
    D. Sloane Stephens

6. Who won the men's singles title at the French Open in 2019?

    A. Novak Djokovic
    B. Roger Federer
    C. Rafael Nadal
    D. Stan Wawrinka

7. Which player won the women's singles title at the French Open in 2020?

A. Iga Świątek
   B. Sofia Kenin
   C. Simona Halep
   D. Garbiñe Muguruza

8. Who won the men's singles title at the French Open in 2021?

   A. Novak Djokovic
   B. Rafael Nadal
   C. Dominic Thiem
   D. Stefanos Tsitsipas

9. Which player won the women's singles title at the French Open in 2022?

   A. Iga Świątek
   B. Barbora Krejčíková
   C. Simona Halep
   D. Naomi Osaka

10. Who won the men's singles title at the French Open in 2023 when they defeated Casper Ruud in the final?

    A. Carlos Alcaraz
    B. Novak Djokovic
    C. Rafael Nadal
    D. Daniil Medvedev

11. Which player won the women's singles title at the French Open in 2023?

    A. Iga Świątek
    B. Emma Raducanu
    C. Leylah Fernandez
    D. Naomi Osaka

12. Who won the men's singles title at the French Open in 2024?

    A. Carlos Alcaraz
    B. Novak Djokovic
    C. Rafael Nadal
    D. Daniil Medvedev

13. Which player won the women's singles title at the French Open in 2024?

    A. Aryna Sabalenka
    B. Emma Raducanu

- C. Leylah Fernandez
- D. Jessica Pegula

14. How many times did Rafael Nadal win the French Open men's singles title between 2004 and 2024?

    A. Ten
    B. 12
    C. 14
    D. 16

15. Who won the men's singles title at the French Open in 2015?

    A. Stan Wawrinka
    B. Rafael Nadal
    C. Andy Murray
    D. Roger Federer

16. Which player won the women's singles title at the French Open in 2014?

    A. Maria Sharapova
    B. Serena Williams
    C. Simona Halep
    D. Petra Kvitová

17. Who won the men's singles title at the French Open in 2010?

    A. Rafael Nadal
    B. Roger Federer
    C. Novak Djokovic
    D. Andy Murray

18. Which player won the women's singles title at the French Open in 2006?

    A. Justine Henin
    B. Serena Williams
    C. Maria Sharapova
    D. Amélie Mauresmo

Chapter 27 Answers:

1. B. Rafael Nadal. Nadal won the men's singles title at the French Open in 2005, marking his first Grand Slam victory.
2. A. 2013. Serena Williams won her third French Open singles title in 2013.
3. A. Stan Wawrinka. Wawrinka won the men's singles title at the French Open in 2016, defeating Novak Djokovic in the final.
4. B. Two. Maria Sharapova won two French Open singles titles between 2004 and 2024.
5. A. Simona Halep. Halep won the women's singles title at the French Open in 2018, marking her first Grand Slam victory.
6. C. Rafael Nadal. Nadal won the men's singles title at the French Open in 2019, in a thrilling final against Dominic Thiem.
7. A. Iga Świątek. Świątek won the women's singles title at the French Open in 2020, her first Grand Slam victory.
8. A. Novak Djokovic. Djokovic won the men's singles title at the French Open in 2021, marking his second victory at the tournament.
9. A. Iga Świątek. Świątek won the women's singles title at the French Open in 2022, marking her second Grand Slam victory.
10. B. Novak Djokovic. Djokovic won the men's singles title at the French Open in 2023, defeating Casper Ruud in the final.
11. A. Iga Świątek. Świątek won the women's singles title at the French Open in 2023, marking her third Grand Slam victory.
12. A. Carlos Alcaraz. Alcaraz won the men's singles title at the French Open in 2024, defeating Alexander Zverev in the final.
13. A. Aryna Sabalenka. Sabalenka won the women's singles title at the French Open in 2024, marking her first Grand Slam victory.
14. C. 14. Rafael Nadal won the French Open men's singles title 14 times between 2004 and 2024.
15. A. Stan Wawrinka. Wawrinka won the men's singles title at the French Open in 2015, defeating Novak Djokovic in the final.
16. A. Maria Sharapova. Sharapova won the women's singles title at the French Open in 2014, marking her fifth Grand Slam victory.
17. B. Roger Federer. Federer won the men's singles title at the French Open in 2010, completing his career Grand Slam.
18. A. Justine Henin. Henin won the women's singles title at the French Open in 2006, marking her fifth Grand Slam victory.

Did You Know?

The 2024 French Open awarded more than 53 million Euros as prize money for the tournament.

CHAPTER 28:
MODERN AUSTRALIAN OPEN

1. Who won the men's singles title at the Australian Open in 2008, his first win at that event?

    A. Roger Federer
    B. Novak Djokovic
    C. Rafael Nadal
    D. Andy Murray

2. In which year did Serena Williams win her seventh Australian Open singles title?

    A. 2015
    B. 2016
    C. 2017
    D. 2018

3. Who won the men's singles title at the Australian Open in 2012?

    A. Andy Murray
    B. Novak Djokovic
    C. Rafael Nadal
    D. Roger Federer

4. How many Australian Open singles titles did Maria Sharapova win between 2004 and 2024?

    A. Zero
    B. One
    C. Two
    D. Three

5. Which player won the women's singles title at the Australian Open in 2018?

    A. Caroline Wozniacki
    B. Serena Williams
    C. Simona Halep
    D. Angelique Kerber

6. Who won the men's singles title at the Australian Open in 2019?

    A. Novak Djokovic
    B. Roger Federer
    C. Rafael Nadal
    D. Dominic Thiem

7. Which player won the women's singles title at the Australian Open in 2020?

    A. Sofia Kenin
    B. Naomi Osaka
    C. Simona Halep
    D. Ashleigh Barty

8. Who won the men's singles title at the Australian Open in 2021?

    A. Novak Djokovic
    B. Rafael Nadal
    C. Daniil Medvedev
    D. Stefanos Tsitsipas

9. Which player won the women's singles title at the Australian Open in 2021?

    A. Naomi Osaka
    B. Ashleigh Barty
    C. Sofia Kenin
    D. Aryna Sabalenka

10. Who won the men's singles title at the Australian Open in 2022?

    A. Rafael Nadal
    B. Novak Djokovic
    C. Roger Federer
    D. Dominic Thiem

11. Which player won the women's singles title at the Australian Open in 2022?

    A. Ashleigh Barty
    B. Naomi Osaka
    C. Simona Halep
    D. Sofia Kenin

12. Who won the men's singles title at the Australian Open in 2023, his tenth victory at the event?

    A. Novak Djokovic
    B. Rafael Nadal
    C. Daniil Medvedev
    D. Carlos Alcaraz

13. Which player won the women's singles title at the Australian Open in 2023, her first Grand Slam victory?

    A. Aryna Sabalenka
    B. Naomi Osaka
    C. Ashleigh Barty
    D. Iga Świątek

14. How many times did Novak Djokovic win the Australian Open men's singles title between 2004 and 2024?

    A. Eight
    B. Nine
    C. Ten
    D. 11

15. Who won the men's singles title at the Australian Open in 2016?

    A. Novak Djokovic
    B. Rafael Nadal
    C. Andy Murray
    D. Roger Federer

16. Which player won the women's singles title at the Australian Open in 2015?

    A. Serena Williams
    B. Maria Sharapova
    C. Simona Halep
    D. Victoria Azarenka

17. Who won the men's singles title at the Australian Open in 2010?

    A. Roger Federer
    B. Rafael Nadal
    C. Novak Djokovic
    D. Andy Murray

18. Which player won the women's singles title at the Australian Open in 2008?

    A. Maria Sharapova
    B. Serena Williams
    C. Justine Henin
    D. Venus Williams

Chapter 28 Answers:

1. B. Novak Djokovic. Djokovic won the men's singles title at the Australian Open in 2008, marking his first Grand Slam victory. He has won a total of ten Australian Open titles and 24 Grand Slam singles titles in his career.
2. C. 2017. Serena Williams won her seventh Australian Open singles title in 2017. She won a total of 23 Grand Slam singles titles in her career.
3. B. Novak Djokovic. Djokovic won the men's singles title at the Australian Open in 2012, marking his third victory at the tournament.
4. B. One. Maria Sharapova won one Australian Open singles title between 2004 and 2024. She won a total of five Grand Slam singles titles in her career.
5. A. Caroline Wozniacki. Wozniacki won the women's singles title at the Australian Open in 2018, marking her first Grand Slam victory. She won one Grand Slam singles title in her career.
6. A. Novak Djokovic. Djokovic won the men's singles title at the Australian Open in 2019, marking his seventh victory at the tournament.
7. A. Sofia Kenin. Kenin won the women's singles title at the Australian Open in 2020, marking her first Grand Slam victory. She has won one Grand Slam singles title in her career.
8. A. Novak Djokovic. Djokovic won the men's singles title at the Australian Open in 2021, marking his ninth victory at the tournament.
9. A. Naomi Osaka. Osaka won the women's singles title at the Australian Open in 2021, marking her fourth Grand Slam victory. She has won a total of four Grand Slam singles titles in her career.
10. A. Rafael Nadal. Nadal won the men's singles title at the Australian Open in 2022, defeating Daniil Medvedev in the final. He won a total of 22 Grand Slam singles titles in his career.
11. A. Ashleigh Barty. Barty won the women's singles title at the Australian Open in 2022, marking her third Grand Slam victory. She retired in 2022 and won a total of three Grand Slam singles titles in her career.
12. A. Novak Djokovic. Djokovic won the men's singles title at the Australian Open in 2023, marking his tenth victory at the tournament.
13. A. Aryna Sabalenka. Sabalenka won the women's singles title at the Australian Open in 2023, marking her first Grand Slam victory. She has won a total of two Grand Slam singles titles in her career.

14. C. Ten. Novak Djokovic won the Australian Open men's singles title ten times between 2004 and 2024.
15. A. Novak Djokovic. Djokovic won the men's singles title at the Australian Open in 2016, marking his sixth victory at the tournament.
16. A. Serena Williams. Williams won the women's singles title at the Australian Open in 2015, marking her 19th Grand Slam victory. She won a total of 23 Grand Slam singles titles in her career.
17. A. Roger Federer. Federer won the men's singles title at the Australian Open in 2010, marking his fourth victory at the tournament. He retired in 2022 and won a total of 20 Grand Slam singles titles in his career.
18. A. Maria Sharapova. Sharapova won the women's singles title at the Australian Open in 2008, marking her third Grand Slam victory. She won a total of five Grand Slam singles titles in her career.

Did You Know?

The 2025 Australian Open awarded more than 96 million Australian dollars in prize money.

CHAPTER 29:
MODERN OLYMPIC TENNIS

1. Who won the men's singles gold medal at the 1996 Atlanta Olympics?

    A. Andre Agassi
    B. Sergi Bruguera
    C. Leander Paes
    D. Marc Rosset

2. In which year did Venus Williams win her first Olympic gold medal in women's singles?

    A. 2000
    B. 2004
    C. 2008
    D. 2012

3. Who won the men's singles gold medal at the 2008 Beijing Olympics?

    A. Roger Federer
    B. Rafael Nadal
    C. Novak Djokovic
    D. Andy Murray

4. How many Olympic gold medals did Serena Williams win in women's doubles between 1996 and 2024?

    A. Two
    B. Three
    C. Four
    D. Five

5. Which player won the women's singles gold medal at the 2016 Rio Olympics?

    A. Serena Williams
    B. Angelique Kerber
    C. Monica Puig
    D. Garbiñe Muguruza

6. Who won the men's singles gold medal at the 2012 London Olympics?

    A. Novak Djokovic
    B. Rafael Nadal
    C. Andy Murray
    D. Juan Martín del Potro

7. Which player won the women's singles gold medal at the 2020 Tokyo Olympics?

    A. Naomi Osaka
    B. Belinda Bencic
    C. Ashleigh Barty
    D. Simona Halep

8. Who won the men's singles gold medal at the 2024 Paris Olympics?

    A. Novak Djokovic
    B. Carlos Alcaraz
    C. Daniil Medvedev
    D. Alexander Zverev

9. Which country won the most Olympic tennis medals between 1996 and 2024?

    A. United States
    B. Great Britain
    C. Spain
    D. Russia

10. Who won the women's singles gold medal at the 2004 Athens Olympics?

    A. Justine Henin
    B. Serena Williams
    C. Maria Sharapova
    D. Venus Williams

11. Which player won the men's singles gold medal at the 2000 Sydney Olympics?

    A. Yevgeny Kafelnikov
    B. Andre Agassi
    C. Roger Federer
    D. Marat Safin

12. Who won the women's singles gold medal at the 2008 Beijing Olympics?

    A. Serena Williams
    B. Venus Williams
    C. Maria Sharapova
    D. Elena Dementieva

13. Which player won the men's singles gold medal at the 2016 Rio Olympics?

    A. Novak Djokovic
    B. Rafael Nadal
    C. Andy Murray
    D. Juan Martín del Potro

14. How many Olympic gold medals did Venus Williams win in women's singles between 1996 and 2024?

    A. One
    B. Two
    C. Three
    D. Four

15. Who won the women's singles gold medal at the 1996 Atlanta Olympics?

    A. Steffi Graf
    B. Monica Seles
    C. Lindsay Davenport
    D. Arantxa Sánchez-Vicario

16. Which player won the men's singles gold medal at the 2004 Athens Olympics?

    A. Roger Federer
    B. Rafael Nadal
    C. Nicolás Massú
    D. Andy Roddick

17. Who won the women's singles gold medal at the 2012 London Olympics?

    A. Serena Williams
    B. Maria Sharapova
    C. Victoria Azarenka
    D. Petra Kvitová

18. Which player won the men's singles gold medal at the 2020 Tokyo Olympics?

    A. Novak Djokovic
    B. Alexander Zverev
    C. Daniil Medvedev
    D. Stefanos Tsitsipas

Chapter 29 Answers:

1. A. Andre Agassi. Agassi won the men's singles gold medal at the 1996 Atlanta Olympics, defeating Sergi Bruguera in the final.
2. A. 2000. Venus Williams won her first Olympic gold medal in women's singles at the 2000 Sydney Olympics. She won a total of four Olympic gold medals in her career.
3. B. Rafael Nadal. Nadal won the men's singles gold medal at the 2008 Beijing Olympics, defeating Fernando González in the final.
4. C. Four. Serena Williams won four Olympic gold medals in women's doubles between 1996 and 2024.
5. C. Monica Puig. Puig won the women's singles gold medal at the 2016 Rio Olympics, defeating Angelique Kerber in the final.
6. C. Andy Murray. Murray won the men's singles gold medal at the 2012 London Olympics, defeating Roger Federer in the final.
7. B. Belinda Bencic. Bencic won the women's singles gold medal at the 2020 Tokyo Olympics, defeating Markéta Vondroušová in the final.
8. A. Novak Djokovic. Djokovic won the men's singles gold medal at the 2024 Paris Olympics, defeating Carlos Alcaraz in the final.
9. A. United States. The United States won the most Olympic tennis medals between 1996 and 2024.
10. A. Justine Henin. Henin won the women's singles gold medal at the 2004 Athens Olympics.
11. A. Yevgeny Kafelnikov. Kafelnikov won the men's singles gold medal at the 2000 Sydney Olympics, defeating Tommy Haas in the final.
12. D. Elena Dementieva. Dementieva won the women's singles gold medal at the 2008 Beijing Olympics, defeating Dinara Safina in the final.
13. C. Andy Murray. Murray won the men's singles gold medal at the 2016 Rio Olympics, defeating Juan Martín del Potro in the final. He won a total of two Olympic gold medals in his career.
14. A. One. Venus Williams won one Olympic gold medal in women's singles between 1996 and 2024.
15. C. Lindsay Davenport. Davenport won the women's singles gold medal at the 1996 Atlanta Olympics, defeating Arantxa Sánchez-Vicario in the final.
16. C. Nicolás Massú. Massú won the men's singles gold medal at the 2004 Athens Olympics, defeating Mardy Fish in the final.
17. A. Serena Williams. Williams won the women's singles gold medal at the 2012 London Olympics, marking her first Olympic victory.

18. B. Alexander Zverev. Zverev won the men's singles gold medal at the 2020 Tokyo Olympics, defeating Karen Khachanov in the final.

Did You Know?

As of 2025, Great Britain has collected 43 total medals in Olympic tennis, two more than the United States.

CHAPTER 30:
MODERN DAVIS CUP

1. Which country won the Davis Cup in 1993?

    A. United States
    B. Sweden
    C. Russia
    D. Germany

2. In which year did Spain win their first Davis Cup title?

    A. 1998
    B. 1999
    C. 2000
    D. 2001

3. Which of these countries won the Davis Cup in 2008?

    A. Spain
    B. United States
    C. Russia
    D. Czech Republic

4. How many Davis Cup titles did France win between 1994 and 2024?

    A. One
    B. Two
    C. Three
    D. Four

5. Which country won the Davis Cup in 2016?

    A. Argentina
    B. Croatia
    C. Great Britain
    D. Switzerland

6. Who won the Davis Cup in 2010?

    A. Serbia
    B. Spain
    C. Czech Republic
    D. Russia

7. Which country won the Davis Cup in 2021?

    A. Spain
    B. Russia
    C. France
    D. Canada

8. Who won the Davis Cup in 2013?

    A. Czech Republic
    B. Spain
    C. Switzerland
    D. France

9. Which country won the Davis Cup in 2015?

    A. United States
    B. Great Britain
    C. Australia
    D. France

10. Who won the Davis Cup in 2024?

    A. Italy
    B. Spain
    C. Russia
    D. France

11. Which country won the Davis Cup in 2004?

    A. Spain
    B. Croatia
    C. Russia
    D. United States

12. Who won the Davis Cup in 2018?

    A. Croatia
    B. Spain
    C. Switzerland
    D. Argentina

13. Which country won the Davis Cup in 1995?

    A. United States
    B. Sweden
    C. Germany
    D. Australia

14. How many Davis Cup titles did Spain win between 1994 and 2024?

    A. Four
    B. Five
    C. Six
    D. Seven

15. Who won the Davis Cup in 2009?

    A. Spain
    B. United States
    C. Russia
    D. France

16. Which country won the Davis Cup in 2014?

    A. Czech Republic
    B. Spain
    C. Switzerland
    D. France

17. Who won the Davis Cup in 2002?

    A. United States
    B. Sweden
    C. Germany
    D. Russia

18. Which country won the Davis Cup in 1997?

    A. United States
    B. Sweden
    C. Germany
    D. Australia

Chapter 30 Answers:

1. D. Germany. Germany won the Davis Cup in 1993, marking their first victory in the competition since West Germany won twice in 1988 and 1989.
2. C. 2000. Spain won their first Davis Cup title in 2000, defeating Australia in the final.
3. A. Spain. Spain won the Davis Cup in 2008, defeating Argentina in the final.
4. C. Three. France won three Davis Cup titles between 1994 and 2024. They won in 1996, 2001, and 2017.
5. A. Argentina. Argentina won the Davis Cup in 2016, marking their first victory in the competition. They defeated Croatia in the final.
6. A. Serbia. Serbia won the Davis Cup in 2010, defeating France in the final.
7. B. Russia. Russia won the Davis Cup in 2021, marking their third victory in the competition.
8. A. Czech Republic. Czech Republic won the Davis Cup in 2013, defeating Serbia in the final.
9. B. Great Britain. Great Britain won the Davis Cup in 2015, marking their tenth victory in the competition.
10. A. Italy. Italy won the Davis Cup in 2024, defeating Netherlands in the final.
11. A. Spain. Spain won the Davis Cup in 2004, marking their second victory in the competition.
12. A. Croatia. Croatia won the Davis Cup in 2018, defeating France in the final.
13. A. United States. United States won the Davis Cup in 1995, defeating Russia in the final.
14. C. Six. Spain won six Davis Cup titles between 1994 and 2024, with the most recent victory occurring in 2019.
15. A. Spain. Spain won the Davis Cup in 2009, defeating the Czech Republic in the final.
16. C. Czech Republic. Czech Republic won the Davis Cup in 2013, defeating Serbia in the final.
17. D. Russia. Russia won the Davis Cup in 2002, defeating France in the final.
18. B. Sweden. Sweden won the Davis Cup in 1997, defeating the United States in the final.

Did You Know?

Since 1972, the United States has collected nine Davis Cup titles, closely followed by Sweden, who has seven.

CHAPTER 31:
ATP AND WTA FINALS

1. Who won the ATP Finals men's singles title in 1995?

    A. Pete Sampras
    B. Boris Becker
    C. Andre Agassi
    D. Michael Stich

2. In which year did Martina Hingis win her first WTA Finals singles title?

    A. 1997
    B. 1998
    C. 1999
    D. 2000

3. Who won the ATP Finals men's singles title in 2003?

    A. Roger Federer
    B. Andy Roddick
    C. Lleyton Hewitt
    D. David Nalbandian

4. How many ATP Finals men's singles titles did Novak Djokovic win from 1994 to 2024?

    A. Five
    B. Six
    C. Seven
    D. Eight

5. Which player won the WTA Finals singles title in 2008?

    A. Serena Williams
    B. Venus Williams
    C. Jelena Janković
    D. Caroline Wozniacki

6. Who won the ATP Finals men's singles title in 2016?

    A. Andy Murray
    B. Roger Federer
    C. Rafael Nadal
    D. Stan Wawrinka

7. Which player won the WTA Finals singles title in 2017?

    A. Caroline Wozniacki
    B. Simona Halep

    C. Garbiñe Muguruza
    D. Elina Svitolina

8. Who won the ATP Finals men's singles title in 2020?

    A. Novak Djokovic
    B. Daniil Medvedev
    C. Alexander Zverev
    D. Stefanos Tsitsipas

9. Which player won the WTA Finals singles title in 2021?

    A. Garbiñe Muguruza
    B. Ashleigh Barty
    C. Naomi Osaka
    D. Simona Halep

10. Who won the ATP Finals men's singles title in 2022?

    A. Novak Djokovic
    B. Daniil Medvedev
    C. Carlos Alcaraz
    D. Jannik Sinner

11. Which player won the WTA Finals singles title in 2022?

    A. Caroline Garcia
    B. Iga Świątek
    C. Aryna Sabalenka
    D. Coco Gauff

12. Who won the ATP Finals men's singles title in 2023?

    A. Novak Djokovic
    B. Daniil Medvedev
    C. Carlos Alcaraz
    D. Jannik Sinner

13. Which player won the WTA Finals singles title in 2024?

    A. Iga Świątek
    B. Aryna Sabalenka
    C. Coco Gauff
    D. Jessica Pegula

14. How many ATP Finals men's singles titles did Roger Federer win between 2000 and 2012?

- A. Four
- B. Five
- C. Six
- D. Seven

15. Who won the ATP Finals men's singles title in 2005?

    - A. David Nalbandian
    - B. Rafael Nadal
    - C. Andy Roddick
    - D. Nikolay Davydenko

16. Which player won the WTA Finals singles title in 2010?

    - A. Serena Williams
    - B. Kim Clijsters
    - C. Caroline Wozniacki
    - D. Victoria Azarenka

17. Who won the ATP Finals men's singles title in 2013?

    - A. Novak Djokovic
    - B. Roger Federer
    - C. Andy Murray
    - D. Stan Wawrinka

18. Who won the WTA Finals singles title in 2019?

    - A. Ashleigh Barty
    - B. Naomi Osaka
    - C. Simona Halep
    - D. Elina Svitolina

Chapter 31 Answers:

1. B. Boris Becker. Becker won the ATP Finals men's singles title in 1995. He defeated Michael Chang in the final.
2. B. 1998. Martina Hingis won her first WTA Finals singles title in 1998. She defeated Lindsay Davenport in the final.
3. A. Roger Federer. Federer won the ATP Finals men's singles title in 2003, defeating Andre Agassi in the final. He won a total of six ATP Finals titles in his career.
4. C. Seven. Novak Djokovic won seven ATP Finals men's singles titles between 1994 and 2024.
5. B. Venus Williams. Williams won the WTA Finals singles title in 2008, marking her first victory at the tournament. She defeated Vera Zvonareva in the final.
6. A. Andy Murray. Murray won the ATP Finals men's singles title in 2016, defeating Novak Djokovic in the final.
7. A. Caroline Wozniacki. Wozniacki won the WTA Finals singles title in 2017, marking her first victory at the tournament. She defeated Venus Williams in the final.
8. B. Daniil Medvedev. Medvedev won the ATP Finals men's singles title in 2020, defeating Dominic Thiem in the final.
9. A. Garbiñe Muguruza. Muguruza won the WTA Finals singles title in 2021, her first WTA Finals title. She defeated Anett Kontaveit of Estonia in the final.
10. A. Novak Djokovic. Djokovic won the ATP Finals men's singles title in 2022, defeating Casper Ruud of Norway in the final.
11. A. Caroline Garcia. Garcia won the WTA Finals singles title in 2022, marking her first victory at the tournament. She defeated Aryna Sabalenka in the final.
12. A. Novak Djokovic. Djokovic won the ATP Finals men's singles title in 2023, marking his seventh and final victory at the tournament. He defeated Jannik Sinner in the final.
13. C. Coco Gauff. Gauff won the WTA Finals singles title in 2024, marking her first victory at the tournament. She defeated Zheng Qinwen in the final.
14. C. Six. Roger Federer won six ATP Finals men's singles titles between 2000 and 2012. He retired in 2022 with those six ATP Finals titles.
15. A. David Nalbandian. Nalbandian won the ATP Finals men's singles title in 2005, defeating Roger Federer in the final.

16. B. Kim Clijsters. Clijsters won the WTA Finals singles title in 2010, marking her third and final victory at the tournament. She defeated Caroline Wozniacki in the final.
17. A. Novak Djokovic. Djokovic won the ATP Finals men's singles title in 2013, defeating Rafael Nadal in the final.
18. A. Ashleigh Barty. Barty won the WTA Finals singles title in 2019, marking her first victory at the tournament. She defeated Elina Svitolina in the final.

Did You Know?

The 2024–2026 WTA Finals will take place in Riyadh, Saudi Arabia on hard courts. They will award $15.25 million.

CHAPTER 32:
DOUBLES RECORDS

1. Which men's doubles team is the only duo to have won two Career Grand Slams in the Open Era?

    A. Bob Bryan and Mike Bryan
    B. Todd Woodbridge and Mark Woodforde
    C. Ken McGregor and Frank Sedgman
    D. John Newcombe and Tony Roche

2. In which year did Martina Navratilova and Pam Shriver complete their first Career Grand Slam in women's doubles?

    A. 1982
    B. 1984
    C. 1986
    D. 1988

3. Who is the only men's doubles team to achieve a Grand Slam?

    A. Bob Bryan and Mike Bryan
    B. Todd Woodbridge and Mark Woodforde
    C. Ken McGregor and Frank Sedgman
    D. John Newcombe and Tony Roche

4. How many consecutive major titles did Martina Navratilova and Pam Shriver win in women's doubles?

    A. Six
    B. Seven
    C. Eight
    D. Nine

5. Which player has won the most Grand Slam doubles titles in men's tennis?

    A. Bob Bryan
    B. Mike Bryan
    C. Todd Woodbridge
    D. John Newcombe

6. Who is the only women's doubles team to complete the Career Super Slam, which includes an Olympic gold medal and year-end championship?

    A. Serena Williams and Venus Williams
    B. Martina Navratilova and Pam Shriver
    C. Barbora Krejčíková and Kateřina Siniaková
    D. Gigi Fernández and Natasha Zvereva

7. Which men's doubles team holds the record for the longest title streak in major history?

    A. Bob Bryan and Mike Bryan
    B. Todd Woodbridge and Mark Woodforde
    C. Ken McGregor and Frank Sedgman
    D. John Newcombe and Tony Roche

8. Which of these was the first women's doubles team to achieve the Career Golden Slam?

    A. Serena Williams and Venus Williams
    B. Martina Navratilova and Pam Shriver
    C. Barbora Krejčíková and Kateřina Siniaková
    D. Gigi Fernández and Natasha Zvereva

9. Which player has won the most Grand Slam doubles titles in women's tennis?

    A. Martina Navratilova
    B. Pam Shriver
    C. Serena Williams
    D. Venus Williams

10. Who is the only men's doubles team to complete a non-calendar year Grand Slam?

    A. Bob Bryan and Mike Bryan
    B. Todd Woodbridge and Mark Woodforde
    C. Ken McGregor and Frank Sedgman
    D. John Newcombe and Tony Roche

11. Who is the only women's player to complete a Calendar Grand Slam in doubles during the Amateur Era?

    A. Christine Truman
    B. Darlene Hard
    C. Margaret Osborne duPont
    D. Maria Bueno

12. Who was the first men's doubles team to complete the Career Super Slam?

    A. Bob Bryan and Mike Bryan
    B. Todd Woodbridge and Mark Woodforde
    C. Ken McGregor and Frank Sedgman
    D. John Newcombe and Tony Roche

13. Which player has won the most Grand Slam mixed doubles titles?

    A. Martina Navratilova
    B. Margaret Court
    C. Bob Bryan
    D. Mike Bryan

14. How many Grand Slam doubles titles did Serena Williams win in her career?

    A. 12
    B. 14
    C. 16
    D. 18

15. Which women's doubles team won six straight major titles as part of their non-calendar year Grand Slam?

    A. Serena Williams and Venus Williams
    B. Martina Navratilova and Pam Shriver
    C. Barbora Krejčíková and Kateřina Siniaková
    D. Gigi Fernández and Natasha Zvereva

16. Which men's doubles team holds the record for the most Grand Slam titles in the Open Era?

    A. Bob Bryan and Mike Bryan
    B. Todd Woodbridge and Mark Woodforde
    C. Ken McGregor and Frank Sedgman
    D. John Newcombe and Tony Roche

17. Which mixed doubles team is the only one to ever achieve a true Grand Slam?

    A. Margaret Court and Ken Fletcher
    B. Billie Jean King and Owen Davidson
    C. Martina Navratilova and Bob Bryan
    D. Gigi Fernández and Todd Woodbridge

18. Margaret Osborne duPont and Louise Brough won 20 doubles titles at Grand Slam events. How many of those 20 wins came at the U.S. Open?

    A. Six
    B. Eight
    C. Ten
    D. 12

Chapter 32 Answers:

1. A. Bob Bryan and Mike Bryan. The Bryan brothers completed their second Career Grand Slam in 2013 at the French Open.
2. B. 1984. Martina Navratilova and Pam Shriver completed their first Career Grand Slam in women's doubles in 1984 with a win at the French Open.
3. C. Ken McGregor and Frank Sedgman. McGregor and Sedgman are the only men's doubles team to achieve a Grand Slam, winning all four major titles in a single calendar year in 1951.
4. C. Eight. Martina Navratilova and Pam Shriver won eight consecutive major titles in women's doubles, the all-time record.
5. B. Mike Bryan. Bryan has won the most Grand Slam doubles titles in men's tennis, with 18 titles.
6. C. Barbora Krejčíková and Kateřina Siniaková. Krejčíková and Siniaková are the only women's doubles team to complete the Career Super Slam. They completed the feat in 2022 with a win at the U.S. Open.
7. C. Ken McGregor and Frank Sedgman. The team holds the record for the longest title streak in major history, with seven consecutive titles from the 1951 Australian Open to the 1952 Wimbledon Championships.
8. A. Serena Williams and Venus Williams. The Williams sisters completed the feat in 2001, and again in 2010.
9. A. Martina Navratilova. Navratilova has won the most Grand Slam doubles titles in women's tennis, with 31 titles. The next closest players only have 21.
10. A. Bob Bryan and Mike Bryan. The Bryan brothers won all four majors in a row but over the course of two calendar years.
11. D. Maria Bueno. She won all four majors in doubles play during the 1960 calendar year. Because she had two different partners during those wins, she is the only player in Amateur Era history with the doubles Grand Slam.
12. B. Mark Woodforde and Todd Woodbridge. The two players completed the Career Super Slam with the 2000 French Open, eight years after their first major win at the 1992 Australian Open.
13. B. Margaret Court. Court has won the most Grand Slam mixed doubles titles, with 21 titles. Seven of those titles came during the Open Era.
14. B. 14. Serena Williams won 14 Grand Slam doubles titles in her career.

15. D. Gigi Fernández and Natasha Zvereva. The two women won each major from the 1992 French Open to the 1993 Wimbledon Championships.
16. A. Bob Bryan and Mike Bryan. The Bryan brothers hold the record for the most Grand Slam titles in men's doubles in the Open Era with 16 titles.
17. A. Margaret Court and Ken Fletcher. The pair won every major championship in 1963.
18. D. 12. Their 12 titles remain the most by any women's doubles team in tennis history.

Did You Know?

Martina Hingis achieved a doubles Grand Slam in 1998, though she used two different partners to achieve the feat.

CHAPTER 33: WOMEN'S RECORDS

1. Which player holds the record for the most Grand Slam singles titles in women's tennis?

    A. Serena Williams
    B. Steffi Graf
    C. Margaret Court
    D. Chris Evert

2. In which year did Steffi Graf achieve the Golden Slam, winning all four majors and the Olympic gold medal?

    A. 1984
    B. 1988
    C. 1992
    D. 1996

3. Who holds the record for the longest winning streak in women's Open Era competition?

    A. Martina Navratilova
    B. Steffi Graf
    C. Serena Williams
    D. Chris Evert

4. How many Grand Slam singles titles did Serena Williams win in her career?

    A. 20
    B. 21
    C. 22
    D. 23

5. Which player has won the second-most Grand Slam singles titles in the Open Era?

    A. Martina Navratilova
    B. Steffi Graf
    C. Margaret Court
    D. Chris Evert

6. Who holds the record for the most consecutive Grand Slam singles titles in women's tennis?

    A. Martina Navratilova
    B. Steffi Graf
    C. Serena Williams
    D. Chris Evert

7. Which player has won the most WTA Tour titles in women's tennis?

   A. Martina Navratilova
   B. Steffi Graf
   C. Serena Williams
   D. Chris Evert

8. Who holds the record for the most Grand Slam singles finals appearances in women's tennis?

   A. Serena Williams
   B. Steffi Graf
   C. Chris Evert
   D. Martina Navratilova

9. Which player has won the most Grand Slam singles titles at a single tournament in women's tennis?

   A. Serena Williams
   B. Steffi Graf
   C. Margaret Court
   D. Chris Evert

10. Serena Williams is tied with which player for the record of most consecutive weeks at No. 1 in the WTA rankings?

    A. Lindsay Davenport
    B. Steffi Graf
    C. Martina Navratilova
    D. Chris Evert

11. Which player has won the most Grand Slam singles titles on clay courts in women's tennis?

    A. Serena Williams
    B. Steffi Graf
    C. Chris Evert
    D. Martina Navratilova

12. Who holds the record for the most Grand Slam singles titles played on grass courts in women's tennis?

    A. Serena Williams
    B. Steffi Graf
    C. Margaret Court
    D. Martina Navratilova

13. Which player has won the most Grand Slam singles titles on hard courts in women's tennis?

    A. Serena Williams
    B. Steffi Graf
    C. Chris Evert
    D. Martina Navratilova

14. How many Grand Slam singles titles did Helen Wills win in her career?

    A. 16
    B. 17
    C. 18
    D. 19

15. Which of these players has not achieved a streak of six consecutive Grand Slam tournament wins, amateur or Open Era?

    A. Maureen Connolly
    B. Margaret Court
    C. Steffi Graf
    D. Martina Navratilova

16. Who holds the record for the most Grand Slam singles titles in the Open Era without achieving a Calendar Grand Slam?

    A. Serena Williams
    B. Steffi Graf
    C. Margaret Court
    D. Chris Evert

17. Who holds the record for the most Grand Slam singles titles in women's tennis before the Open Era?

    A. Margaret Court
    B. Helen Wills Moody
    C. Maureen Connolly
    D. Suzanne Lenglen

18. Serena Williams and Martina Navratilova both won how many Grand Slam tournaments without losing a single set?

    A. Four
    B. Five
    C. Six
    D. Seven

Chapter 33 Answers:

1. C. Margaret Court. Court holds the record for the most Grand Slam singles titles in women's tennis, with 24 titles.
2. B. 1988. Steffi Graf achieved the Golden Slam in 1988, winning all four majors and the Olympic gold medal.
3. A. Martina Navratilova. Navratilova holds the record for the longest winning streak in the Open Era, with 74 consecutive match wins.
4. D. 23 titles. Serena Williams won 23 Grand Slam singles titles in her career.
5. B. Steffi Graf. She won 22 Grand Slam titles in her career, one behind Serena Williams.
6. A. Martina Navratilova. She won six straight Grand Slam titles, the most someone can win without completing a Grand Slam.
7. A. Martina Navratilova. Navratilova has won the most WTA Tour titles in women's tennis, with 167 titles.
8. C. Chris Evert. Evert holds the record for the most Grand Slam singles finals appearances in women's tennis, with 34 finals.
9. C. Margaret Court. Court has won the most Grand Slam singles titles at a single tournament in women's tennis, with 11 titles at the Australian Open.
10. B. Steffi Graf. Graf and Williams share the record for the most consecutive weeks at No. 1 in the WTA rankings, with 186 weeks each.
11. C. Chris Evert. Evert has won the most Grand Slam singles titles on clay courts in women's tennis, with seven titles at the French Open.
12. D. Martina Navratilova. Navratilova holds the record for the most Grand Slam singles titles on grass courts in women's tennis, with nine titles at Wimbledon.
13. A. Serena Williams. Williams has won the most Grand Slam singles titles on hard courts in women's tennis, with 13 titles.
14. D. 19 titles. Her last win came at the Wimbledon Championships in 1938.
15. C. Steffi Graf. She only had a streak of five Grand Slam wins, ending with the 1989 Australian Open.
16. A. Serena Williams. Williams has won the most Grand Slam singles titles in the Open Era without achieving a Calendar Grand Slam.
17. B. Helen Wills Moody. Moody holds the record for the most Grand Slam singles titles in women's tennis before the Open Era, with 19 titles.

18. C. Six tournaments. Both women achieved the feat six times in the Open Era. Helen Wills Mcody did it 13 times in the Amateur Era.

Did You Know?

Steffi Graf reached 13 straight Grand Slam finals from 1987 to 1990, and Martina Navratilova is second on that list with 11 straight appearances from 1985 to 1987.

CHAPTER 34:
UNBEATABLE RECORDS

1. Which men's player holds the record for the most Grand Slam singles titles in tennis history?

    A. Pete Sampras
    B. Roger Federer
    C. Novak Djokovic
    D. Rafael Nadal

2. In which year did Rod Laver achieve his Calendar Grand Slam?

    A. 1962
    B. 1965
    C. 1969
    D. 1972

3. Who holds the record for the longest match in tennis history?

    A. Roger Federer vs. Rafael Nadal
    B. John Isner vs. Nicolas Mahut
    C. Novak Djokovic vs. Andy Murray
    D. Björn Borg vs. John McEnroe

4. How many Grand Slam singles titles did Rafael Nadal win at the French Open?

    A. Ten
    B. 11
    C. 12
    D. 14

5. Which of these players has not won five U.S. Open titles?

    A. Jimmy Connors
    B. Pete Sampras
    C. Roger Federer
    D. John McEnroe

6. Who is tied with Stan Smith for the most Davis Cup titles as a player?

    A. Bill Johnston
    B. Bill Tilden
    C. Roy Emerson
    D. Norris Williams

7. Which player has won the most ATP Tour titles in men's tennis?

    A. Roger Federer
    B. Jimmy Connors

C. Rafael Nadal
   D. Novak Djokovic

8. Who holds the record for the most Fed Cup titles as a player?

   A. Chris Evert
   B. Martina Navratilova
   C. Serena Williams
   D. Billie Jean King

9. Which player has won the most Grand Slam singles titles at a single tournament in tennis history?

   A. Serena Williams
   B. Roger Federer
   C. Margaret Court
   D. Rafael Nadal

10. Who holds the record for the most consecutive weeks at No. 1 in the ATP rankings?

    A. Roger Federer
    B. Novak Djokovic
    C. Pete Sampras
    D. Rafael Nadal

11. Which player has won the most Wimbledon Championships singles titles in men's tennis history?

    A. Novak Djokovic
    B. Roger Federer
    C. Pete Sampras
    D. Rafael Nadal

12. Who holds the record for the most Grand Slam women's singles titles at Wimbledon in tennis history?

    A. Serena Williams
    B. Helen Wills
    C. Margaret Court
    D. Martina Navratilova

13. Margaret Court won 603 matches on which court type?

    A. Carpet
    B. Clay
    C. Hardcourt
    D. Grass

14. How many Grand Slam titles did Roger Federer win in his career?

    A. 18
    B. 20
    C. 22
    D. 24

15. Who holds the record for the most ATP Masters 1,000 titles in men's tennis?

    A. Roger Federer
    B. Rafael Nadal
    C. Novak Djokovic
    D. Andre Agassi

16. Which women's player has won the most titles in a single year during the Open Era?

    A. Billie Jean King
    B. Margaret Court
    C. Martina Navratilova
    D. Chris Evert

17. Who holds the record for the most Olympic medals in tennis?

    A. Serena Williams
    B. Venus Williams
    C. Steffi Graf
    D. Rafael Nadal

18. How many times did Rafael Nadal lose when reaching a French Open final?

    A. Zero
    B. One
    C. Two
    D. Three

Chapter 34 Answers:

1. C. Novak Djokovic. His 24 singles titles are the most among men's players and tied with Margaret Court on the ladies' side.
2. C. 1969. Rod Laver achieved his Calendar Grand Slam in 1969, winning all four majors in a single calendar year. He remains the only men's player to achieve the feat.
3. B. John Isner vs. Nicolas Mahut. Isner and Mahut hold the record for the longest match in tennis history, lasting 11 hours and five minutes at Wimbledon in 2010.
4. D. 14. Rafael Nadal won 14 Grand Slam singles titles at the French Open.
5. D. John McEnroe. He is tied with Rafael Nadal and Novak Djokovic with four U.S. Open titles each.
6. C. Roy Emerson. Emerson and Smith hold the record for the most Davis Cup titles as a player, with eight titles.
7. B. Jimmy Connors. Connors has won the most ATP Tour titles in men's tennis, with 109 titles. Roger Federer is in second place on the list with 103 wins.
8. A. Chris Evert. Evert is the only player to win the tournament eight times in her career.
9. D. Rafael Nadal. Nadal's 14 French Open titles is the most by any player at any Grand Slam tournament.
10. B. Novak Djokovic. Djokovic holds the record for the most consecutive weeks at No. 1 in the ATP rankings, with 428 weeks.
11. B. Roger Federer. He won the Wimbledon Championships eight times in his career.
12. D. Martina Navratilova. Navratilova holds the record for the most Wimbledon Championships titles in women's tennis history, with nine.
13. D. Grass. She won almost 200 more matches on grass than the next player on the list, Billie Jean King.
14. B. 20. Roger Federer won 20 Grand Slam singles titles in his career.
15. C. Novak Djokovic. Djokovic holds the record for the most ATP Masters 1,000 titles in men's tennis, with 40 titles.
16. B. Margaret Court. She won 21 titles in 1970. She also holds second and third place on the all-time list with two different years of 18 wins each.
17. B. Venus Williams. Williams holds the record for the most Olympic medals in tennis, with four gold medals and one silver medal.

18. A. Zero. Rafael Nadal reached the French Open final 14 times, and each time he emerged victorious.

Did You Know?

Bill Tilden's winning percentage of 89.76 is the best of all time, with Djokovic in third place, winning 88.02 percent of his matches.

CONCLUSION

There you have it, another match has reached its conclusion, and this one was a marathon! You likely needed more than five hours to finish the questions in these pages, which would make it one of the longest tennis matches in history!

You also likely saw many names you didn't recognize, so now you have plenty of motivation to learn more about the sport you love. There were big names making big waves on courts around the world, even before the Open Era came to be.

Even more exciting is that tennis history is being written every year! Will anyone catch Novak Djokovic's records? Regardless, there's no doubt that with each serve, volley, lob, and spike, players will continue to battle to reach the top of the tennis world.

Until then, this book will help you continue learning about the champions of the past. Keep working on that backhand as you continue to review the questions and answers in this book!

www.ingramcontent.com/pod-product-compliance
Lightning Source LLC
Chambersburg PA
CBHW060458030426
42337CB00015B/1640